Smile!

Animal Antics

Edited by
Helen Davies

First published in Great Britain in 2011 by:
Forward Poetry
Remus House
Coltsfoot Drive
Peterborough
PE2 9BF
Telephone: 01733 890099
Website: www.forwardpoetry.co.uk

Book Design by Spencer Hart

SB ISBN 978-1-84418-571-9

Foreword

Animal Antics 2011 sees the return of one of our most popular recurring themes here at Forward Poetry - poems inspired by animals from across the globe.

Within these pages you'll see why creatures great and small are so inspiring to the poetic mind and creative hand. How our best friends and confidantes can be furry or scaly; how our inner well-being can be nourished by observing the animal kingdom in all its glory; how our curiosity is often ignited by the lives of fantastical and faraway creatures.

As always, the selection process was a very enjoyable experience, as the contributors skilfully share their heartfelt thoughts in verse: sometimes comedic, sometimes in remembrance, and often with accompanying photos to make their words come to life.

After flipping through this rewarding collection, we're sure you'll agree - wouldn't life be quiet and boring without animals to brighten up our days!

Contents

The Poems

Liza – Where The Kites Are

Coming with us across the fields towards the shore,
she's already hanging back, lagging behind, bringing up the rear
at a safe distance. She'd rather not be here at all.
We turn and see her watching kites, head forward,
ears down, knowing we'll call her and hitch the lead to her collar.
Reluctantly she closes in, anxiety brimming, knowing we shall go
where the kites are.

Her sight is deteriorating, her hearing
isn't good but she knows before we do,
the kites are out. They sweep low, swinging above
the hedge, rising again, soaring, rumbling,
their puffed-up breasts cradling the wind beneath them.
She wants to make a run for it and thinks she might,
but loyalty persuades her to stay with us, though fearing to go
where the kites are.

Windsurfing enthusiasts out on the water, leap
and swing, relishing the risks they take,
defying fear. Wires rattle, the sea is boisterous,
splashing, splattering, bumping, lifting the boards as they ride
the waves, oblivious of the torment they are causing our poor dog.
She wishes she was somewhere else, anywhere but here,
where the kites are.

After five minutes we turn for home. I'm holding the lead.
She takes off at speed, towing me after her. There's
no lagging behind now, she has the energy of two
and my legs move faster than they have in years.
Up the bank and over the track, across the park
and into the field where, encouraged by her successful escape,
she allows her tail to swing, allows me to rest and look back
to see the others laughing, hurrying to join us from the shore,
where the kites are.

Rosa Johnson

From Becky On Father's Day

I won't be there at playtime
For our fights upon the floor,
And I won't be there to greet you
As you open the front door.
I know that you will miss me
Though you fight hard to be brave,
But you were right to let me go
I was far too ill to save,
I didn't want to leave you
But the time had come to go,
You did your best to help me
And to ease the pain I know.
I think about you all the time
And all the fun we had
And how I'm always happy
Because I had you for my dad
Please don't fret about my going
Though I may seem far away
I'm here with Sam and having fun
Each day's a lovely day

The fields are green,
There're things to chase
I don't feel any pain
Although I want to be with you
I can't come back again
I want to send you all my love
And barks and kisses too
And wish you happy Father's Day
And remember if you're blue
I'm here with Sam and all the rest
The dogs you've known through life
Waiting the day, however long
When you and your dear wife
Come here to find and join us
And happy then we'll be
Together, all forever
In the green fields, running free.

J Gartside

My Pet

My dog Brandy is four years old,
When I took her on she was as good as gold!

I taught her agility and lots of tricks,
And I praise her with toys and sticks!

When we got her she was only a puppy,
And she was always getting really mucky!

I like to give her bones and treats,
And other stuff she likes to eat!

She loves to go and get really wet,
But she doesn't like her trips to the vet!

When I go out she waits at the gate,
And sometimes stays there till really late!

I love my dog, she's my best friend,
But sometimes drives me around the bend!

My dog will leave hairs on my bed, mud in my kitchen, but no matter what . . .
She will always leave a paw print in my heart!

Shannon Smith

Dexter

You came into my life on just the right day
Melted my heartstrings straight away
Tiny and tense you shook with fear
Nuzzled my neck and nibbled my ear
Too small to walk, I carried you around
When I sat, you slept, ignoring any sound
My little treasure is a beautiful boy
His presence brings me unbelievable joy
For many a year I lived in fear of leaving my home
Crippling panic kept me a prisoner indoors
Taking my time I now venture out more and more
You have given me a reason to live each day
Not sit in my chair and fade away
I hate to be parted from this little chap
He offers me comfort from any mishap
Small in body but big in mind
To me and my family he is always kind
My mother has Alzheimer's but loves my little lad
The smile on her face means a lot to my dad
He takes away the tension and confusion that she feels
His soft and gentle nature temporarily heals
He takes me to the field where he plays chase the ball
He forgets to bring it back; still you cannot have it all
This bundle of fun fills every day
My mini Jack Russell is never in the way
He walks with a strut and a proud little grin
I cannot imagine my life without him.

Lynn Elizabeth Noone

My Precious

Some say cats are smelly, boring, silly,
But nothing can amount to my cat Ziggie,
He's loyal and nice, not to mention cute,
He's sweet and soft, much like a fruit.

I could hug him all day, every single night,
I could listen to him purr in the daylight,
I'd tell him each day in every sentence that I say;
'Ziggie, without you I wouldn't be here to this day.'

Whatever bad news is said on TV every morn,
I know Ziggie will enlighten me with a stroke of scorn,
It's like we have a connection, one that's very strong,
His bed next to mine is one where he belongs.

Do you want to know how Ziggie got his name?
It wasn't just because it was from a man of fame,
The first day he came home, he sat on this top,
Ziggie's Shirt, it said, so we knew it was his prop.

Ziggie's my boy; he's my special boy
He loves a fuss and a little mouse toy,
Whenever he's not around I mope for a while,
But when he is around he makes both of us smile!

Georgia Hargreaves (13)

A Poem About My Cat

Delicately
with such elegance
and ever so slowly
she laps up her milk
out of her saucer
with her sandpaper tongue.

Quietly
Oh so slyly
stealthily and silent
Pounce!
Upon a hugely terrifying . . .
cushion.

Needfully
filled with jealousy
she purrs
jumps on your lap
if she is not the centre
of your attention

Lovingly
brimming with care
she nuzzles your neck
if you're upset
she curls up on your bed
and makes everything feel just fine.

Niamh Lily Jarvis-Smith (13)

Timothy Tubby Cat

When you arrived you were thin and poor
Sitting forlorn just beyond my door,
A cut on your head which was sore and bleeding
and an empty tum which needed feeding
I cleaned up your wounds and gave you some meat
Groomed you and wormed you, which was no easy feat
You jumped on the table out on the lawn
and stayed there from dusk right through to dawn
Over the days you became very brave
and love and company you started to crave
I caught you and took you to visit the vet
I think you were the loveliest cat they had met!
No teeth, cross-eyed, short ears, FIV
But handsome and wonderful you looked to me
So my gummy little pal you became a house cat
And every evening since on my knee you have sat
When night-time comes you sleep on my bed
In the mornings you wake me as you want to be fed
I thank the Powers that be every single day
that you came to me and wanted to stay
Timothy Tubby Cat you're a wonderful friend
and I'll love and care for you right up to the end.
You started to act strangely, I knew something was wrong
As when I woke in the morning, from the bed you had gone
I'd find you lying on a cold floor
Or sitting patiently by the back door.
I took you to the vet to allay my fear
And they told me something I didn't want to hear.
A tumour was growing inside your tum
and I realised a decision time had come
Soon the vets will operate on you
And again, I pray that you would pull through
I expected to bring you home last night
But what the vet saw wasn't a good sight
The phone call came and the news was sad
The tumour was large and the cancer was bad
I raced to your side, my face covered in tears
You woke and purred as I stroked your ears
Then slowly and quietly you went to sleep
Leaving me alone, without you, to weep.

Angela Baines

Biscuits

Oscar Sprocker.
Part springer,
Part cocker,
Always hungry.

Wakes early morning,
Springs upstairs,
Scratches door,
No one cares.
They're half-asleep,
Snoozing soundly,
Opens mouth,
Starts barking loudly.
Grumbles sound,
They come around,
Woken by that blasted hound.
Fall out of bed,
They dress and clean.
They follow the school day routine.

All in the kitchen
Ready for school,
Breakfast served,
Oscar drools.
A cupboard clicks,
A tin bowl clatters,
Ears perk up.
Nought else matters.
They fill the bowl
And close the door.
Oscar sits down
On the floor.

Heartbeat rises,
Breathing slows,
Tongue licks his lips,
His snout and nose.
Tail freezes still
As tin meets tile.
They stand,
He waits
For a while.
Silence falls,
Time seems to slow,

The command is given:
'Oscar, go!'
Head rushed down,
Towards the ground,
Mouth open wide.

Biscuits.

Daniel Ford

The Cat That Sat On The Mat

The cat that sat on the mat.
And meow'd and meow'd,
very loud . . .
at 5am,
just when,
I'd got asleep.
This cat, I do not keep . . .
It keeps me!
For I cannot tame.
Only when, to be fed, will she answer to her name . . .
Twinkle Toes.
With a twitch of her nose,
off she goes,
into the shadows . . .
Quickly to disappear
Taking forever to return.
Only manipulative tricks, does she learn.
Won't wait.
Won't come.
Scratching at invisible, balls spun.
Gradually, the furniture is ripped to a shred.
Again, demands to be fed.
Then content, curls up, with elastic spine.
To soak up the bathroom window sill's sunshine.
Catnap . . .
Later.
On all fours,
paws and claws,
wiggles her backside, in my face, then ignores . . .
But I still love my pussycat.
For I must enjoy, being used as a doormat.

Tony Chestnut Brown

She was like a piece of black wind,
The white tip of her tail above the long grass.
Even her conversation was small, only when necessary.
But good things never last, never at all.

Beside me, carving our initials with my brother's penknife,
Careful of the blade, she danced around the bark,
Seven and nine years of age.

I never dreamt of today,
When our paces are much the same,
Yet her coat is what compliments her;
Her son, looking old enough to be his mother's grandfather.

We stroll by the ash tree, loyal companion and me,
I glance at where I once used that knife,
The engravings have grown, like us.
But we remain close, the whole rest of our lives.

Caoimhe Tully (16)

Cat Poem

I blow a raspberry at you, I'm not directing Cat Balou,
A film director's life is stress, a catnap is due I must confess.
Maybe the Rat Pack would be good to screen,
Or Mickey Mouse with footage unseen.
Rewrite a role for Pussy Galore, I'll purr and hiss or lash out with paw.
By a whisker an Oscar for the team,
Miaows all round for the cat that got the cream.
I'm busy I must go, my next film's a spoof,
From 1958, Cat On A Hot Tin Roof.
Rocky Moggiano.

John Ward

Tickles

So needy are those eyes
Glaring out from inside the cage
But I know if I open the door
There would really be a rage

My budgie who I call Tickles
Always expects a lot more
But one sniff of the outside world
And a commotion would arise for sure

A ladder, some toys and a swing
Fresh water and plenty of seed
But it doesn't appear to be enough
To fulfil his increasing need

To cut a long story short
It really does drive one insane
That each time Tickles comes out
He flies straight at the windowpane

Which is why I am so reluctant
To open the door and see
My beloved pet budgie Tickles
Lying sprawled out in front of me.

Sarah Mears

Bracken

Amber eyes glint mischievously at a pheasant waddling around the leaf litter.
A sleek black mantle that glistens in the morning sun as it drives away the darkness of night.
A wet nose searches through emerald fern and mahogany
pine needles, bleeding an auburn-coloured sap.
We blow sharp whistles for her to return and she lopes from the
bushes unperturbed from the shrill shrieks of the buzzards.
Jumping head first, she crashes into the silky blue river, clenching
the stick in her jaws she obediently returns to the shore.
Oblivious to the freezing cold, she throws herself into the air to catch a pure white snowball.
This is Bracken, our energetic, crazy, black Lab.

Jasper Farren (11)

He came to us, eight weeks
Of age, a jolly, happy lad.
But as he got to know us, he
Began to get rather bad!

He'd climb our legs and eat our
Laces, and just get in the way.
Soon Dad was threatening to
Have him sent away.

We persevered with our new friend,
And every day we walked
A fair distance and of course at first
He was good - but not later on.

He'd run away, dash and play,
In ways that he should not.
For chasing trains is really
Not the best pastiming plot.

His train chase kept for a year and a half.
Till one snowy day at the park.
One last chase did Benson go
But it threw him into eternal dark.

His ashes were scattered at a protective pine,
Where at his best he loved to run,
Chasing birds and
Foxes, having great fun.

Those days after Benson's death,
The way I felt I'll try and tell.
It felt as though within my heart,
A major support beam had been cracked.

The house was strange,
It wasn't home,
So we decided on another dog,
To get that silence begone.

So into our lives,
After months of searching,
Carly came
On Mum's knee perching.

A tiny tot,

Young and scared,
But never
Have her teeth been bared.
We watched her learn,
We watched her grow,
We think of him and
Miss him so.

Carly's kind, Carly's
Good, but I hope he understood.
She's not to
Replace him, nothing could.

He's always in our heart,
And I think that,
Had they ever met,
Carly and he would be like whisker and cat.

Isla Scott (12)

Dogs

Dogs are clean, dogs are dirty,
They bark too much, it makes me crazy,
They have fur tails, soft and silky,
They sit in their baskets, whining and sobbing.

Different dogs, different sizes,
They hide under tables and down the back alleys.
They run in the parks and back to their owners,
They cuddle up tight all ready to sleep.

Ashika Gauld

Canine Comfort

Your love is totally unconditional
You sit loyally by my side each day
And when I put my arms around you
Your warmth melts my worries away

I treasure our special companionship
You're always there as my friend
Uncomplicated and non-judgmental
Devoted and faithful till the end.

Anniko Kevin

Mojo

Well here it is Mo, the time has come,
Our last goodbye, your last run.
This wasn't supposed to happen so soon,
You're still supposed to be in my room.
I know we've had our ups and downs,
But Mojo you were the best of hounds.
You were my best mate, my best friend for life,
Through everything, all the pain and strife.
I know if you can hear me you won't understand a word,
But the point is so I know that you've heard.
Heard my voice and heard us here,
Sorry we're not all applauds and cheers.
But Mojo you know this is going to be hard,
No more birthdays, no more cards.
I'm going to miss you more than anything, I hope you know it's true,
And Jake and I were talking and our little brother is you.
We all love you so much, you were our protector,
A right little bugger, a real energy injector.
Until your last few days when you started to slow down,
But it was still fun to have you around.
You know unconditional love pets have for their owners,
Well we had it for you so maybe that makes us loners.
But who cares? I don't and certainly does no one else here,
As we knew you and have reason to love thee who deserves a cheer.
We will remember the good times and laugh upon the bad,
But please do notice we will be unbearably sad.
For we have not just lost a family pet dog,
But a family member, a winding cog.
It will take time to accept you're gone,
But you will forever and always be our shining sun.

I love you Mojo xx

Ashleigh Frances Atherton

Gone Too Soon

It seems no time at all since when
You brought them home with you,
You trained them, cherished them and then
You watched them as they grew.

You thought you had a lifetime long,
To live and love and play,
And suddenly, it feels so wrong
That they've been snatched away.

Those few short days were all you had,
The angels called too soon,
The hope, the joy seem now so sad,
A snapshot, flower-strewn.

What happened to those happy years,
The summers in the sun?
All washed away in grief and tears,
Before they had begun.

There must have been a purpose here,
Although you've had to part,
And you will keep your memories near,
As solace for your heart.

Brenda Maple

Chuff's Dream

Snoozing by the fireplace,
Content as a cat can be,
Dreaming of a distant land,
Where pussies alike are free.

Scampering high,
Lost amongst the clouds,
Following a trail of kitten treats,
Jumping with great leaps and bounds.

Crashing onto a hidden beach,
Scampering quickly over the shore,
Staring up at the pile
Of food and treats galore!

Creeping slowly, getting closer,
Towards the tower of food,
He gobbles it up,
Now that was good!

He runs around for a while,
Chasing his tail,
Until he runs head first
Into a solid, golden rail.

'Now Chuff,' the guard says,
'It's time for you to go,
Back to the land of realism
Because your little girl loves you so.'

Charley Zollinger (14)

Giving You The Will To Live

Ever since I saw you
I've sensed that beneath
All the aggressive bluster
Lies a sensitive soul,
In need of love;
Perhaps it is self-identification
On my part.

You were not like the average canine male,
Yes the testosterone was there, certainly,
Even a certain bad temper but
Whenever I let you loose in the paddock
Expecting you to wildly roam beyond recall,
You kept coming back to me
As if deeply insecure,
Seeking a friend's reassurance;

Your past has turned you into a lonely dog,
On the defensive, again all my self-identification reigns but
It helped me take a shine to you,
Wanting to be your friend;
And it seems you have a soft spot for me:
You have bitten all of your various kennel partners
At the rescue kennel;
Re-homed only once
You bit your new owner! (and were returned)
But you have never even growled at me -
I feel honoured.

On my every visit to the kennels
Each time you saw me
You bounced so high in your run
I always feared for your safety (or escapeology),
But your new-found energy
Heartened me also (I had created it)
As I remembered our first encounter
When I only thought of
Giving you the will to live -
Now you have it in abundance!

I once had another greyhound like you:
Aggressive, short-tempered
Nasty to other dogs
(Unless they were mine);
Some called him 'a bully'
But like you again
He loved me to fuss him
And maybe that's another piece of magic
With you - even therapy too -
The bond that we have formed
Takes me back to a happier time,
Better days - and so
Wanting to give you the will to live
Perhaps I was unknowingly striving
To give it to myself as well,
Almost in need as much as you;
Two kindred spirits
May be the secret of our success,
Giving each other a wish to carry on.

Tyrone Dalby

The Homesick Marsupial

I'm a sociable marsupial named Sue
And I'm a new arrival at the zoo.
A jackass took one look, said, 'What are you?'
'I'm a kangaroo, how do you do?
I'm very friendly even though I'm new
Although I must confess to being blue
I miss Australian animals I knew;
Wallabies, koalas and a cockatoo.

So in a zoo like this, there'll be a few
Compatriots of mine to take me to
But Caribou and Marabou won't do
Nor silly hens that cock-a-doodle-doo.
Antipodean animals it's true
Make all the other animals taboo
Especially sheep, who get our grass to chew
So sheep and rams are definitely Non-U.'

The jackass and the homesick kangaroo
Began their search when there came into view
A hairy herbivore, so up spoke Sue,
'I'm a kangaroo, how do you do?'
It said, 'You've pinched my line - I'm a gnu!
I understand you're looking round the zoo
For animals that come from where you do
Please follow me, I know the best venue.

We're off to see the crocodile that slew
Crocodile hunters by the retinue
He made his name and proved the film's untrue
Crocodile Dundee met his Waterloo!
So Bruce the croc is Aussie through and through.
Please follow me to the rendezvous.
We're off to see the lizard,
The wonderful lizard of Oz!'

Chris King

The Wisdom Of Sheep

Sheep are stupid - right?
Or - like us, individuals -
Differing attitudes.

Ewes as mothers - vary
Some good - feed their lambs often,
Others - concentrate on self.

Just like humans - bring
Wisdom and sense to the group,
Reasoning, caring.

Danger comes as fox -
Wise flock closes - protecting,
Young, old - together.

Ram enjoys friendship,
Ewes and lambs - a family bond,
Constant companions.

Lookout ever watching,
Alerts flock to shepherd's call,
Bringing food and care.

Moving field to field,
Flock knows journey and progress,
Can find its own way.

Sheep are stupid? - No,
Watch them emanate wisdom.
There if you but look.

Chris Sangster

For Sally

(Response to the novel 'Love That Dog')

I read the
book you
sent home
with me

the yellow
book with
blue writing
on its pages

As I read I
thought, *how cute* and
wondered why you'd
hugged it to your
chest and
looked as if you'd
cried over it.

and by page 14
I could see
because I was
crying
but only a little

I loved his
vulnerability
and plus it was
really late at night

and by page 27
I was crying
harder
but it was nothing like when
I got to page 44
and he was
talking about
the two reasons
he loved the poem

and tears were
streaming down
my cheeks
as I met Sky
on pages 46 and 47

and on page 64
I laughed out loud
when I read the
poem about his
brain feeling like a
squashed pea

I've felt
that way before

And when I read
pages 68 and 69
and 70 and 71
and 72
my tummy
felt funny and my
throat ached and I
sobbed and sobbed

and then I
lay down on the
floor with
my head resting
on my dog

and her hair
stuck to my
wet face
and she licked at
the salt
and I didn't want
to read anymore
but I couldn't stop there

The poem on page 86
was sad and
sweet
just like the
whole book

and I was glad I read it
I thought about
how it was
really late at night
and I knew that
even if I read
this book in the
middle of the day
I'd still cry.

Christel Ruddy

Our Cat Jimmy 22\11\10

Suddenly there was a silence, a stillness in the house,
A quietness seemed to echo, stirring not even a mouse,
An emptiness, a presence was obviously missing,
Yes, it was our loveable cat Jimmy, his purr was missing.
Today at 2pm Jimmy left our family home,
Wrapped in a blanket, snug and warm, he would no longer roam,
Rosario, our friendly vet had called to take Jimmy away,
His illness had developed complications, this was a very sad day,
We would miss his friendly greeting on returning home,
His gently purr as if to say, 'I didn't like being here alone,'
He would wake us in the morning with a friendly facial paw,
As if saying rise and shine, this is only my friendly call.

He would tell us when he thought it was time for bed,
'Come along then Jimmy,' he'd race ahead covering every tread.
He would closely watch us, as if feeling tension in the air,
Knowing what we had in mind, I'd wonder did he offer up a prayer?
His affectionate nature we will always remember with love,
For he added something special to our lives, known as a friendly buzz,
Often we would say, 'Jimmy, has made a comfortable parcel,'
Nestled outside, watching through the window we tried not to startle.

When he was younger and full of 'get up and go', he would catch mice,
He'd rush down the garden path as if he'd visited paradise,
Mealtimes there was always a place for Jimmy, he had his own plate,
You see Jimmy was a valued member of our family, this is a sad date,
The memories he has left behind will remain with us each day,
His friendly manner, his company, showing how he loved to play.

He shared an understanding of a unique quality of family unity,
Which has been a valued gift to our family, a loving eulogy. xxx

Lorna Tippett

After Passing

(Dedicated to my cats)

Just me again, alone with my thoughts,
When mercurial as slippery shadows,
You appear to me, two haunting sprites,
To replay memories of your devoted loyalties -
My dearly loved though now departed pets.

Diana Kwiatkowski Rubin

My Little Dog

My voice to him is music,
His tail in tempo waves,
Sometimes when he is very bored,
How badly he behaves.
He would follow me to Heaven
And the ends of this great Earth.
Maybe ... he is a little dog ... but,
No wealth could buy his worth.

If humankind could learn from him
His love and faithfulness,
When I can't spend the day with him
He loves me nonetheless.
When I am away from him;
He curls up on the floor,
When I return he wags his tail
And greets me at the door.

I will always love my little dog
I will love him to the end,
And I am very, very proud,
To say ... he's my best friend.

Stephanie Foster

My Monty RIP

My favourite pet sadly died long since,
an Olde English sheepdog was he,
gentle to the end of his thirteen years,
best friend and adoring loyal company.

Daft as a brush, brain limit was small,
But such an affectionate friend,
He'd hear me coming in from work
And bark in raptures, 'til in the end

I had to feed him to hush him down,
so very excitable was he
that the person coming in to fuss him lots
was *his* best friend and owner - me.

He loved to raid my kitchen bin
or snatch biscuits from the plate,
he made his own 'programme' for garden use -
was clean and prompt, never too late

Until he got poorly when in his old age
and found it hard to 'hold on',
then he'd bark and bark 'til I opened the door
whatever the hour; and then he was gone

To water the tree as fast as he could
(but sometimes forgot which leg
to raise to relieve himself - quick!
then he'd turn to *look* at his back and beg!)

Dear ol' Monty, my best pal ever,
he's now on his doggy cloud nine;
he may not have been the cleverest dog
but I was his friend and he mine.

God bless you still my Monty.

Ann Voaden

Animals

I'm only a harmless creature
I've got feelings just like you,
So why do they keep me locked up
In a place they call the zoo?

I'd love to have my freedom
To roam over the country wide
But they've locked up all the gateways
To keep me and my pals inside.

One day the gates may be open
And we will be free to roam
But we will still be strangers
For we are so far from home.

Pat Adams

Harley - The Kamikaze Kitten

He jumps from the sideboard, he swings from the shelves
He climbs up the curtains. In all things he delves.
He speeds up the lounge like a thundering horse
One day he will do himself mischief, of course.

He annoys and pesters our poor old cat, Patch
Who for speed and acrobatics he is more than a match.
Poor Bonnie gets jumped on - she snarls and growls
But Kamikaze Kitten just sits there and howls.

He's nosy, he's naughty, he scratches the chairs
As he runs round and round and then up the stairs.
To catch him is clever, it's become quite an art
For speed and for cunning he has quite a good start.

I watch the TV, drink my lemon barley
Whilst there on my lap curls a kitten called Harley.
He's sweet when he's cuddly, which is not all the time.
But this Kamikaze Kitten is a favourite of mine.

Jennie Rippon

Paddy paws
And waggy tails;
A 'welcome home'
That never fails.

They'll give to you . . .

Smiling eyes
(that don't tell lies)
but comfort
If the need arise . . .

All these pleasures
Wrapped in fur
For us to brush
On him or her . . .

Walkies; playtimes;
Hours of fun
Make you feel
Life's just begun . . .

So, someone, somewhere
Hear our prayer;
'Be kind to doggies everywhere
They're precious gifts
From Heaven above
Sent for everyone to love ... '

Edna Sparkes

What Pet Do I Have?

Their carroty skin is streamlined
Their eyes darting eagerly and their mouths close and open
Bubbles envelop them as they wander in their restricted area.
Their fins stand horizontally as they swim in and out of rocky mountains.
What pet do I have?

A fish!

Folabomi Amuludun

They say memories are golden
well maybe this is true
I don't want memories
I just want you,

A billion times I have needed you
a billion times I have cried for you
If love alone could have saved you,
you would never have died.

In life we all loved you dearly,
in death we love you still,
in our hearts you hold a place
that no one could ever fill.

You leave behind your sons and your daughters
and your grandchildren too.
We miss you very much,
as you went too soon,
if tears could build a stairway to Heaven
we would follow you too.
and if our pain could make a lane
we would walk the path to Heaven
and bring you home to us again.

Our family is broken
and nothing seems to be the same
but as we wait for our call,
just to be reunited with you
once again.

Beige we miss you very much,
we love you with all our hearts
love, your family xxxxxx

Tina Holden

Waves of morning darkness grow dim like an ebbing tide
Stars wink translucent, clustered diamonds, in an inky autumn sky
Rippled streams of silver daylight cascade over the braes
The fading laments of night echo in the fox's eerie, haunted cry
As he prowls, solitary, in the sheen of a waning full moon
The dawn chorus brings leafy bowers alive, chirrups flute-like and long
With joy and excitement Bonny, the collie's eyes open wide
Awakened by the harbinger of morning, the robin's dawn song

The farm collie rises to track wild sheep on misted hills
Bonny yawns and stretches, ears alert, the robin is accompanied
by the blackbird, the thrush and the wren
The farm collie soars over dying bracken and rocky, fern-banked burns
While Bonny's hours pass in the haven of home and garden
From snowdrops, daffodils, bluebells to the yellow of
winter jasmine, nine seasons have passed
But with the soul of a pup Bonny yelps, a heart-rending, impatient whine
Which shatters sleep. My dreams hurtle into outer space, a mirage of splintered glass
Head buried under pillow, I mourn daybreaks which used to be mine

To lie warm and snug in bed, an elusive memory of pre-collie days
Already Bonny is primed, anxious to play football, an hourly pastime of fun and glee
On the lawn adorned by brown, red and golden leaves
She has gambolled all year in the company of the springtime bee
And with the swallows of summer, now migrant geese arrive
The robin sings on the fence, scarlet breast puffed out, a Christmas gem
Bonny leaps into the garden, bathed in a moonlit glow. Is her bark
A ballad, a melody, a hymn? No! It is a football anthem!

Jacqueline Bain

My Dog Tess

As I stepped in through the door
I'd always shout her name.
'Tess, Tess, come here Tess.
I am home again.'

Her eyes would sparkle.
Her ears would stand up straight.
Then she would start panting
Because she could not wait.

She'd lick my face.
She'd give me her paw
And I would give her a chew to gnaw.

It broke my heart
As her life came to an end
Because she was my baby
Not just my best friend.

She'd jump and sit upon my knee
She'd only settle
When she was close to me.

Oh, how I miss her
Now she has gone.
She was my dog
My very special one.

Janet Butlin

Monologue Of The Caged Parrot

Speaking to the plants and garden ornaments,
squawking at the barking dog.
Imitating the human voice
until 'hello', 'good morning' and 'good evening'
become your mantra.

Forgotten how to fly and survive,
cracking seeds and gulping water
living a lifestyle of caged comfort.

Jerome Teelucksingh

Cheetah Glow

(The poem is based on the magnificent painting by Stephen Gayford called 'Cheetah Glow')

With those distinctive tear-stained eyes
The cheetah looked around,
With ears alert to realise
Each sudden nearby sound . . .
In hunting mode, the cheetah sensed
Each second one by one,
Alone, aloof and without friends
Beneath the burning sun . . .

The sizzling light shone down all day,
Upon the cheetah's fur,
To warm its cold heart all the way,
Whatever must occur . . .
For cheetahs want to stay alive,
Regardless of the cost . . .
They fight a war so they survive,
Until the war is lost . . .

This cheetah's stare looked left and right,
For something unaware,
Before the creature's taken flight
On land or in the air . . .
As fast as cheetah legs can run,
Starvation is the foe,
Beneath the ever-burning sun
That makes the cheetah glow . . .

Denis Martindale

In Honour Of

A silhouette plays on the wall, the lady of the night has awoken.
She greets the night with familiarity, her oil-black fur blending into darkness.
Her sapphire eyes reflect the full moon and her dainty paws tread with effortless silence.
If you hear a sound, know that it was intentional.

Frolicking in the shadows and consorting with the stars, she makes the night her own.
At the sound of her name a gentle purr emanates from the darkest corner.
She finds enchantment in the simplest of things,
Eyeing the nightlife with a curiosity reminiscent of childhood.

She tells you with a glance that she knows a secret, one you'll probably never know
And a gentle swish of her tail reminds you, you're privileged to gain her attention.
Her stance echoes Bast, an elegance and strength that seems centuries old.
Her will is born out of a wildness that can never truly be broken.

She cannot be owned. Her spirit transcends possession.
You are her carer, her confidant, often her pillow.
She comes to you freely because you have earned her trust and her love
Which are among the greatest gifts she has to bestow.

Erin Fitzgerald

In Loving Memory Of Johnny

This story is about our pet
Who was big and strong and bonnie
He recently has slept away
So let me tell you about Johnny.

We don't know where you came from
On that peaceful starry night
When you wandered in my aunt Kate's door
You must have seen her light

That was over sixteen years ago
And though you were no kitten
You were mature and from the wild
Aunt Kate and I were smitten!

Officially you were her cat
But when she'd visit mine
It couldn't get much better
In two houses you could dine!

So when Auntie would walk over
You'd follow on the tar
But now you were adopted
You would never go too far

If Auntie Kate went to the shop
Along with her you'd go
And no matter where she'd wander
Johnny boy, you'd be in tow!

Johnny boy you were amazing
Only you will know the reason
Why you had so many lovely traits
And how you loved each season.

In the spring you'd love the mornings
You'd smell the sea mist dew
And saunter through the fields of grass
To your own wee private loo!

The summertime you loved boy
You gave yourself the best
The sun's rays streaming from blue skies
Down upon your long grass nest

Animal Antics 2011

In those autumn mild calm evenings
You'd ask out to romance
And all the village female cats
With you they'd want to dance!
And on those cold and wintry nights
Your one and true desire
Was lying stretched out on the rug
At the warmth of the open fire

Sometimes you'd bring home presents
Most times it was a mouse
We'd appreciate that Johnny
Just not dropped in the house!

As you lived upon an island
We know you loved the land
But you also loved the sea air
And rolling in the sand!

You loved the good food always
You had your favourite eats
The Sunday roast and mackerel
And those Thomas seafood treats.

And as the years rolled onwards
You decided to retire
No more mice or beach walks
More time spent at the fire

You still patrolled a smaller beat
Though older you had grown
And made sure, while you were still around
No pretenders to your throne!

But those past few weeks you slowed down
The month it was September
The date it was the 29th
'Twas a Wednesday, I remember.

You enjoyed your usual evening heat
And then went to bed with Kate
But just after seven next morning
We had lost our dear soulmate

For at twenty-five past seven
You were purring, then a sigh
And to our lovely Johnny
We would have to say goodbye

We built your little resting box
We chose to make it pine
Inside it's lined with sheepskin
For a pet who was sublime

Now you rest beneath your rosebush
On your grass path facing west
Thank you for such precious memories
Johnny, simply, you're the best!

Cambi Anderson

Pnut The Pigeon

This is a tale of a rather daft bird,
Who landed in our garden and demanded to be heard,
His wing was badly injured and he looked scared,
So some shelter, food and water were quickly prepared.

We wondered if he would make it through the night,
He was such a small bird and quite a pitiful sight,
Turned out he was a pigeon and I gave him a name,
Pnut he was christened and a feathered friend he became.

He made is home on the garden bench,
I was worried the rain would certainly drench
His little feathers and make him cold,
But for a pigeon he was really very bold.

Pnut sheltered in his plastic box during the day,
He seemed to know he could not fly away,
The other pigeons would come and feed,
Pnut would join them eating seed.

Down from the bench for a drink he would hop,
In the beginning he would land with a flop,
Then using the step and the plant pot,
Up he would jump when he'd eaten his lot.

The back of the bench is where he would roost,
A lovely mess overnight he always produced,
He stayed with us for twelve whole days,
I forever worried about him out there, always.

One day he flew up to the roof from the fence,
That moment was scary and very intense,
He made it and everyone cheered,
I was so worried that day until he reappeared.

Now time has moved on but Pnut is still around,
His brilliant recovery and flying skills do astound,
Each day he comes in for a drink and some food,
Off you fly Pnut, be safe and remember it was here you were rescued.

Marie Date

Untitled

You came over and said, 'Hello,'
I knew then I could never let you go.
I said, 'I'll take that wee one by the chair,'
I just loved your brown eyes and your black velvet hair.
You were so biddable, so loving and so cute,
We even took you down the chute.
My daughter had been mauled,
Looking at her injuries we were appalled.
But you behaved impeccably, you thought you were one of us,
I even paid for a seat for you on the bus.
The doctor did agree,
You were the best dog for me and my three.
RIP Sparky
Gone but never forgotten. xxx

J Forrest

The Black Dog Of Light

His life was one of discontent
His joy hid behind tall trees
Like the moon on a dark night
But when that light shone through
It was the opening to a whole new world
His eyes smiled and the day was brighter
He began to roll and play and my heart smiled
One thing I will never forget
Is no matter how bad I felt
His moments of light
Made me blissful.

Haimanot Haile (17)

Animals (Minus The Cat)

When I was a kid, I wanted this and that,
A rabbit, a hamster, or maybe a cat.
Two out of three wasn't that bad,
Cos a rabbit and hamster is what I had.
Then we had dogs, one or two
Actually it was five, that's quite a few,
We had chicks under a lamp, oh how sweet
My goat had a baby, that was a treat.
A cockerel and chickens in a huge run,
But if I'm honest, they weren't much fun,
We also had ferrets, they were the best ever,
I'd play with them and bite me, they never.
We had racing pigeons in a posh loft
Come racing day, the pigeons were off,
So all in all we had more than two or three
But I never did have that cat you see!

Susan Johnstone

I Stroked A Cat

I stroked a cat. A *very* pleasant cat.
The nicest type you can imagine: slender,
Content and unassuming cat. And yet
She was so warm, so welcoming, so tender -
And so relaxed ... I want to be like her:
Just sit all day under the sun - and purr.
(And never cry - or be distressed - or vexed)
And idly wonder: 'Who will stroke me next?'

Natalia Crofts

Walk With My Friend

I close the door behind me and head off down the track,
My faithful friend looks up at me, pulling at his lead and occasionally looking back,
His excitement has no limits, although he's walked this route before,
His senses working overtime as he sniffs along the floor,
A short time into our journey we stop and take a break,
The constant pulling on the lead has caused my arm to ache,
We find a suitable resting place to sit and drink some tea,
I remove the rucksack from my back and place it on my knee.

Zander's eyes look up at me as he sits around my feet,
He tilts his head to one side and watches what I eat.
His stare is fixed upon my hand as it moves up to my lips,
He salivates uncontrollably as I drink my PG Tips,
I know what's going through his mind, he's waiting for a treat.
Ten minutes pass and we're good to go and spring back to our feet,
So we both stand up, Zander shakes himself as he's chomping at the bit,
His excitement builds once again, so I order him to sit.

We wander off at a steady pace, taking in the view that we've found
Then Zander stops with urgency and looks forward at the ground
I kneel down beside him; hold his collar in my hand
I unbuckle his lead and let him go, then I struggle to try and stand
He's caught sight of a rabbit and goes off in attack
He runs through gorse and bushes, I give him five minutes, then call him back
He never caught that rabbit,
He never does in fact, it's not through lack of trying,
He just doesn't have the knack,
We've been walking for an hour and we're both drenched through to the bone,
I look at Zander tiring so decide to head back home.

Zander's back on the lead as we turn and head for home,
I then receive a message on my mobile phone
'Your dinner's in the oven, make sure you wipe your feet,
I've cleaned the house from top to bottom, it all looks very neat.'
Considering the message, I look down at my friend, I laugh uncontrollably,
He's covered in mud from end to end.
I laugh at him, watching him shiver and his eyes gaze back at me
I then reconsider the message,
There's only one place for him to be.

So, I throw a stick; then he jumps in for a swim,
And when he brings it back, he looks ever so thin.

We have a few more minutes and a little bit more fun,
Then I examine his coat, yep, the washing is done
Back on the lead he shakes himself dry,
It all turns slow motion as I watch the spray fly.
We're back at the house, our walk's at an end,
What a wonderful feeling sharing the day with my best friend.

Dave Gallivan

Snips, Scruffy And Seymour

If dogs and cats were riches, I would have a few,
But if they were sun-drenched days, my skies would be forever blue,
If my days were numbered to the happiest ones spent,
They would be the days I spent fondly with my pets

First came a midnight kitten, gifted on my tenth birthday,
The worry and the hurt I felt when she would go astray,
She climbs in through the window and eats my Sunday chips,
But she eclipses any sadness, my silky sweetheart Snips.

On a crisp October evening, as the winds began to calm,
My poppa came home early, in his dirty workshop van,
He sent me out to fetch a hammer, but I couldn't comprehend why,
For he had never done any chore before he ate his shepherd's pie.

I slid open the rusty door and in the darkened boot,
I saw two unkempt terriers in dire need of food,
Poppa had rescued them from an oncoming ominous fate,
To be drowned in the river down by the creaking gate.

However we had suffered a tragedy or four,
When one day Scruffy took a bite out of Seymour,
Or on the day we spied the limp Scruffy had disguised,
The vet had said he'd injured his skinny scruffy thigh.

But through it all the pups were brave and never lost their spark,
And stayed as bountiful and gay as that night out in the dark,
When they were brought into our life and filled it with such joy,
But now we don't need any more, thankfully they're both boys!

Two dogs and one cat, you would think they had her outnumbered,
But their chasing expertise she has many times encumbered,
Snips is smart and of course elite, they cannot catch her tail,
But of course you could expect no less, for Snips is the female!

Aibhlín Neeson (17)

The Tale Of The Bacon

The little girl skipped down the street to buy a pound of bacon.
Her puppy dog just ran along in case he was forsaken.

The shopkeeper who sold the goods - he was a nice Jamaican
Said, 'Tis de best ting in de morn, a sandwich when you waken.'

The little girl then made to leave, but found herself quite shaken,
For when she went to pick it up, the bacon had been taken.

She said, 'I'm sorry sir, it isn't here. There isn't any bacon.'
The shopkeeper said, 'Oh yes dere is, me know me not mistaken.'

They looked around and soon they found that mischief had been maken.
The puppy dog just rolled his eyes, his guilt now overtaken.

He licked his chops and jumped around, his little tail was shakin'.
He barked out loud then begged for more, he'd so enjoyed the bacon.

David Wall

If I Weren't Human

If I weren't human, tall and proud, here's what I'd rather be;
A tiny little ball of fur, a kitten by a tree.

I'd wobble on my frail legs and jump at every sound,
then pounce on leaves and snowflakes that did fall upon the ground.

Or maybe I'd be full of teeth, a lurking tiger shark.
I'd hunt all day in search of food, just swimming in the dark.

My fin of darkest midnight-blue I'd crest above the wave,
where no one would be brave enough to tell me to behave.

But then again I'd love to glide on thermals in the sky,
and swoop with lazy effortless, an eagle upon high.

With talons sharp and keen of eye I'd spot my latest prey,
then eat enough to satisfy my hunger for the day.

Dickon Springate

My Loyal Friend

Your loyalty is beyond imagination,
Your love needs no explanation.
Simple as girl is to dog,
As dog is to girl.

You wait for me at the door,
You pull me around parks and more.
Simple as girl is to dog,
As dog is to girl.

I give you treats and spoil you so,
You follow me when I say, 'Go!'
Simple as girl is to dog,
As dog is to girl.

When I feel alone you lick my face,
When Mama's not looking you lick my plate.
Simple as girl is to dog,
As dog is to girl.

When rain pours down you don't notice,
When a meal's late you're groaning.
Simple as girl is to dog,
As dog is to girl.

Simple as girl is to dog
As dog is to girl.

Georgie Smith (14)

My Lovely Cat

She hunted for a mouse in my lovely house,
she scratched under my bed for the fearful mouse.
She pounced on her victim with her power and might,
her claws were deadly, she dragged her victim in the night.

She ate her victim and licked her mighty paws,
she crushed the mouse head with her deadly claws.
Her fat belly was filled; she rested on her kitchen mat,
she slept and dreamt of a wonderful bush rat.

She awoke from her rest and beat her fluffy tail,
she jumped on top my table and scratched at my mail.
I heard her cry and wondered what she needs,
I rubbed her brilliant head and sat down to read.

She climbed on top my kitchen wall to hunt again,
she fell down upon the ground when she heard the rains.
I gave her some milk to quench her thirst,
she jumped into her basket and said she was first.

I watched her dream in her sleep and weep,
she folded her hands under her head like a sheep.
You are such a delightful and captivating cat!
You are always on the alert for mischievous rats.

You are my lovely house pet that inspires my heart,
some day you shall be gone for our souls to part.
A lovely fluffy cat like you so clever is hard to find,
you live in my heart and dream; O you are always on my mind!

Gideon Sampson Cecil

My Special Someone

I fell in love with it
Cute as can be
It was sleeping on my lap
I was watching while stroking it carefully
I was told it was a 'he'
And he wasn't friendly to anyone
But you came to me
After a while you woke up again
You raised your head and looked at me
I will never forget those beautiful eyes
You turned your head, following your nose
You spotted my chocolate cake and had a bite
I named you Cookie
Only six months old but you loved chocolate as much as I did
You were sad when I had to go
And happy when I came back to pick you up
Our life together began
And what a funny fellow you were
Sitting at the dining table with us
You had your own chair of course
Using a toothbrush
Or were you just chewing on it?
I caught you running in the washing machine
Don't know where you got that idea from
Following me to the bathroom
And waiting for me outside
When I didn't let you in
You were sleeping in my bed
On my pillow right next to me
We played, we laughed
And you gave me comfort when I was sad
One day I came back from school
But you weren't waiting for me
You were nowhere to be found
Tears were running from my eyes
As I realised what had happened to you
I cried after you died
I cried more because you weren't there to comfort me
You were a member of the family
You were my important friend
I miss you every day
And I will always love you.

Isabel Seidl

Animal Antics 2011

Guinea Pig Rescue

A snuffle and a squeak,
A wiggle and a peek,
Out of the hutch to freedom.

A sniffle and a purr,
A flash of ginger fur,
Out of the hutch to freedom.

A pitter and a patter,
If only she were fatter,
She's out of the hutch to freedom.

A drip and a drop,
Splashing non-stop,
Sitting under the hutch, no freedom.

Raining full pelt,
Fur matted like felt,
It's not how she imagined her freedom.

Curled up and shivering,
Tiny ears all quivering,
Wishing she was warm and safe and dry.

A human hand,
A friendly touch.
A fluffy towel and fluffier fur.
A happy squeak, a happy purr,
Guinea pig rescue complete.

Hester Alderman (17)

Winter Beasts

Winter brings the gentle snow,
And everyone loves it as we know,
Beautiful and crisp clean on the floor,
But that's only until we opened the door,
Thud after thud the sound grew,
Paw after paw pushing through,
Splodges of brown and black amongst white,
Seen in the winter sunlight,
No coat, only fur to keep them warm,
Early in the fresh winter morn,
Bounding about the garden freely,
The dogs having fun so easily,
Time to go out and leave the dogs at home,
Them and their shed and the snow alone,
Saying goodbye to my giant cuties,
Big gentle beasts in the winter beauty.

Katrina Miles (16)

The Crooner

(As a pigeoner I composed this piece of verse about a race in 2005 of about 400 miles against a head wind into Derry City from Portland Bill.)

After six days in the basket
From Portland Bill in 2005
Flying hundreds of miles
To the loft by the back door . . .

On that evening
At approximately seven
Winning club and federation
In fact, the only day arrival
In spite of wind direction.

Yes! A thoroughbred
Intelligent and friendly
With the best of the bloodlines
Of the Jan Aarden dynasty.

Liam Ó Comáin

King Of His Jungle

He lay in wait in the long tall grass
Just waiting for his mate
She walked real close but was unaware
But now it was too late
He leapt from the grass with a lion's roar
She had no time to flee
He was on top of her within a flash
The king of his jungle you see
Holding her firmly within his paws
Beginning to lick her face
The shock of being taken like this
Did make her little heart race
By now she knew who her attacker was
She rolled over and swiped his nose
It was his turn to be surprised
With his hackles up he struck his pose
'Look at me,' he says, 'I am the king of beasts
How dare you strike me down!'
He wagged his tail side to side
She saw his glare and frowned
Walking over to him she rubbed her cheek
Against his little nose so sore
She knew he was just only playing
For soon they would be kittens no more . . .

Kevin Foster

Irreconcilable Difference

Our cat lay down on the grass
Wet, to the touch
Grubby pussy
Meanwhile in the yard
Our dog bared his teeth
Barked loud - hard
Spare us the news
Or the view of the neighbours
The cat or dog spoiling for a fight
All night
A tussle, a hustle, a bustle
Cat chases dog
Poor dog howls in the yard
Cat meanwhile chases the rats
Doggy paws quite sore afflicted
Back comes pussy very sorry
Mixing up the bowls the dishes
Caused Irreconcilable Differences . . .

Stella M Thompson

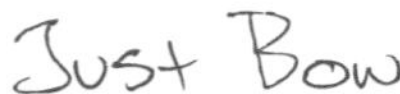

Although he may look dark,
His eyes give out the light,
He may be kind of large,
He is never out of sight.
Although he has a smell,
That only I can bear,
It's one that only I can love,
And always know he's there.
His bear-like walk is quite unique,
To his specific breed,
His slobber can reach a ceiling tall,
To all he can exceed.
But the smell, the door and hair on the floor,
Don't really matter at all,
The thing, he's mine that smelly mutt,
He's my big furry ball.

Kerry Mclean

Puppy Love

So soft,
So huggable,
Terror pots,
Forgivable.

Shiny coats,
Silky paws,
That's what it's all about.

They'll grow up one day,
Leave your side,
That's when you'll notice,
Their big brown eyes.

Their big brown eyes,
Shine right inside,
Right inside . . .
My heart.

Alex Nicole Hall (14)

To Cricket

You like to jump up on the roof
You crazy cat
And run around it all day long.

You get up high as you can
And look all around
Not wanting to be grounded.

You climb up on all the trees
Your own private perch
Never wanting to come down.

Will you ever stay down,
You crazy cat?
Or will you always be high?

Sheila L Drury

Question Time

What are the things at the end of her feet,
Are they toys for play or mice to eat?

What are those things from her ears?
As they swing and dangle there

What are these things tall, like a tree?
Oh no, we've just scratched her knee

What if we kiss her nose,
Will she love us, do you suppose?

What if we take a nap,
Curled up warm upon her lap . . .

Will she keep us?

Anita Richards

My Animals

I've had animals all of my days
Cats and dogs, most of them strays
They come to my door, I let them in
Looking frail and awfully thin
I feed them meat and give them bones
And when they're strong
Send them off to new homes
The latest one, I call him Jake
Maybe making a big mistake
He claws my curtains and claws my chairs
And round the house leaves bright orange hairs
But he is cute and I forgive him his crime
Hope he will settle and I can keep him as mine.

Isabella Erroch

Bert

The love of my life has left me
After thirty beautiful years
We met when I was very young
We shared a lot of tears

The feelings and the memories
Will stay inside my mind
All the things he told me
He was really very wise

We used to share our stories
Before we went to sleep
He used to stay beside me
Like a treasure I did keep

Even though I'll miss him
I know he's somewhere safe
Without my country music
That's one thing he did hate

Oh how I will miss you
My shiny little man
All these years together
Without so much as a frown.

Goodbye Bert
The best tortoise in the world!

Shirley Harrison

Spaniel

With chin gently resting upon my knee
And soft brown eyes gazing up to me
Ever hopeful some time soon
I will get up and leave the room
And take her where she longs to be
Down in the woods running free.

Rabbits, squirrels, pheasants beware
The spaniel is hunting without a care
Her love for life is plain to see
Worldly goods mean nothing to she
All those of us who have lost our way
Sit down and watch the spaniel play.

My loyal companion till the end
Unconditional love and my best friend
Human frailties she does endure with
A knowing look, a comforting paw
I consider it an honour to be
Sharing my life with one such as she.

Louise Pell

Daydream Horse

My horse is as black as a shadow.
She has a long silky mane.
Moonlight's tail is thick and flowing in the rain.
Her eyes are like silver stars sparkling in the dark.
Her hooves are firm as a rock.
Her beautiful nose is as soft as a fluffy white cloud.
She holds her head high, smiling at the sky.
When I ride her I feel I can be anyone I want to be.

Faith Blake (8)

Define A Pet

What makes a pet, a pet?
An animal to own so you do not feel alone?
An ownership or a friendship?
Why small and fluffy? Why not large and fluffy?
Those little questions do not enter your head as you look for a pet to lie on your bed

Gestures show emotions
You always feel loved
Someone that will not push you away or walk away whatever you have to say
Someone to cuddle and make you feel warm
So you will never have to feel alone

They may get up to some mischief
But you really do not care
As long as they are there

My pet is a white little dog
Named after a ghost, he is far from frightening
As he barks to protect us from any dangers there may be ahead
All he asks for in return is a little food as a way to learn

Pets need attention, love and affection
What makes a pet, a pet?
A friendship, not an ownership
They are not just pets.

Lucy Ann Smith (15)

Dudley

Dudley the Dalmatian
You are both companion and pet
Your black and white coat
Makes you stand out from the rest
Early each morning we go
Across fields and through trees
And then down by the railway track
Where you can run fast and free
And then on the way back
Perhaps a swim in the stream
Or a splash around, a frolic
Before coming out and soaking me
I hurl the stick into the distance
And you go hurtling after it
Panting as you return happy
So patiently you wait, you sit
But what I love most ... is
That you are so warm and cuddly
As we lay down by the fire
You are my best friend Dudley.

Craig Shuttleworth

The Ballad Of Balthazar

My rat is of curiosity, a spirit of the mind,
In the darkest of shadows is when his sight is defined,

For you cannot catch a rat that knows more than you,
A rat's life is forever simple as no complications can block its view,

He is more than rodent and too intelligent to be my pet,
And too much of a companion, one worth extending my student debt.

Martin Harrison

My Pals

My guinea pigs are Molly and Peppa,
Ginger and white and brown and cream
They are the most beautiful guinea pigs ever seen.

They love to run, play, squeak and shout
They always know when we're about.
They have a pen in the garden - they play hide-and-seek -
They are not very good - we find them when they squeak

Parsley is their favourite food
It always puts them in a happy mood.
In the winter they come in, sitting on my knee
All three of us then lounge around and watch the TV.

Molly and Peppa - I love them both so very much -
They turn up their igloos in their hutch.
My pals are cheeky, squeaky, fluffy balls of fun
A smile they bring to the face of everyone.

Lucy Reddy (10)

Piglet The Master Huntsman

Each evening at dusk he scrutinises his territory,
His ears point upward to catch any sound
He is ready to prowl, each paw silent, nothing auditory.

Each night he patrols his patch,
Silken paws padding through the damp grass
For he know he has a tasty morsel to catch.

He sniffs the cold dank night air with grace
The prey quite unsuspectingly comes into view
Piglet's pulse and heart begin to race.

No sound must he make lest he frighten
His unsuspecting quarry
He feels every sinew in his body tighten,

His stride quickens as he steals down the path
The creature completely unaware of danger -
Piglet is definitely on the warpath.

He closes in ready to leap
His prey is totally oblivious to the moving threat -
It won't be long until his blood will seep

Into the undergrowth - quick as a flash Piglet pounces
The tiny mouse disappears under the cat's claws,
The battle over; the mighty victor bounces

Back to his hiding place behind the glass
Delicately placing his offering on the mat
Before waiting for another creature to pass.

Patricia J Tausz

Pussycat In The Window

Pussycat in the window
Why won't you come out and play?
You stare at all the passers-by
And lick yourself all day.
We could be chasing insects
And rolling in the grass
We could pretend you're a tiger
But instead you're behind the glass.
Why don't we prowl around and pounce?
We could stalk and run and chase
We could batch a bird, or a mouse
We could have a five-legged race.
While you're sitting in the window
And licking clean your fur
I could teach you how to talk,
You could teach me to purr
And when we've got you nice and clean
And you've learned to talk like me
We could go out to the garden
And climb the biggest tree.

Luna Deller

Farley The Dog

You can smell her before you even enter the room
Even after a bath, a shampoo, and a groom
And I have to say she's not all that pretty
And her temperament not altogether too witty
All she seems to do is sit and lick her chair
And her lady parts and the surrounding hair
But age is no longer on her side
She's just dribbling her way through the rest of the ride
Despite all this her pride is still in place
But sidetracking the elegance and grace
It may not seem like she sounds that great
But I'm hoping all good things come to those who wait.

Sarah McCaffrey

Back To Solo

I'd lived with another being
for four years as of August 19th.
My Bombay cat's been missing
for two weeks as of Sunday.
He's gone away to live
with his wild kitty buddies,
enjoying the bachelor life.
Now I know how divorcees feel.

He comes to visit.
His periodic check
on personal human moments
always occur when my assistants are absent.
He's learned that grabbing a squirming kitty
is beyond my physical capacity.

I miss him, but we both
seem to be doing okay.

Martina Robinson

The Wonky Escape Artist

I once had a fish; it swam leaning,
Must have been a peculiar feeling.
And memory three seconds?
Well, who'd have reckoned?
He always knew when we were cleaning him out

He'd splash and he'd bash in his bowl
Rockin' his whole goldfish soul!
He'd try to escape
And his scaly gold cape
Would flash - he'd be out on a roll!

Jordan Holmes

Jack

Crumpled and creased, he sleeps in the shape of a rugby ball,
His limbs occasionally flailing out like he's doing a parachute jump.
His little nose twitches from time to time and a muffled, squeaky
little bark pops out from behind his closed mouth.
Every once in a while he wakes abruptly,
Sitting bolt upright, expecting to be greeted by an intruder.
His big brown eyes flash towards the wall, the ceiling, the door, then the window.
Confirming his suspicions of an unwelcome guest, he darts
to the open window, giving a bird what for.
Running back and forth, mirroring the bird's flight in the garden, he growls and snarls,
If he could just get out there, he'd catch the damn thing.
When the excitement is over, the bird long gone in the sky,
He looks around helplessly for a new mystery, a new torment.
Unsuccessful, he heads over to his favourite toy, all colourful and chewable.
Wrapping his teeth around its pointy rubber edges, he sets himself yet another mission.
But alas, as his razor-sharp fangs dig into the rubbery, coloured flesh,
His tiresome work is interrupted by a lazy pair of eyes.
His jaw slowly drops the bouncy toy back onto the floor,
Heavy eyelids give in to the tiredness of his hard day.
Contentedly, he lets his little paws stretch out his weary limbs,
Falling onto his side in a blissful, cosy nap.

Sarah Michelle Wilkinson

Pluto

He's the dog of the Underworld, Pluto's his label.
His eyes still alert, are expressive as he looks to the table
Acting out starvation, those jet eyes are silently praying.
He was handsome and black but his muzzle is now greying.

Silence is not one of his best traits at all.
His barking starts sharp and amplifies off the wall.
Someone dares to move outside and staccato sounds hit the ear
Must search eBay for a citronella collar he may learn to fear

If you're working away in your stuffy, office cave,
He's learned he can pester and to make him behave,
He gains handfuls of dog cookies that he won't share with the cat.
The vet says he is not big boned; he's fat!

In the park he wears collars with bling
He's a mini poodle, but he sees himself as king.
It is the jungle and all animals must see him as the lion
And one day some Rottie may send him flyin'!

The bed was never going to be his domain
But at first he was small and not like a Great Dane.
Now he can take over the bed lying sideways with legs sticking out.
and yesterday he even bit me as I slowly tried to get out!

He is wonderful and marvellous that dog in his dotage.
Though knees and back surgery costs have upped my mortgage
He's cost me the Earth in food, grooming and vet fees
But he's my fur kid and I wouldn't swap him for three money trees.

Shirley Baskett

Angel

German Shepherd puppy with ears huge and floppy,
teddy bear coat, I love to stroke.
Lying across my feet, upraised brown eyes I meet,
faithful she will be,
her care, my responsibility.

Softly breathing my little dog sleeps,
Alsatian in miniature growing complete,
a little each day, nature's miraculous way.
Rest my Angel, grow big and strong,
may our lives together be rich and long.

As timeless as love from Creator above,
my Angel and me, loving and free.
Together may we glimpse eternity,
sharing life together in harmony.

Louise Pell

Our Retired Greyhound

Just an old dog who lies on a blanket.
Is that all you see?
There used to be more than this greying muzzle
And elderly frame to me.

Sometimes when I stand at the open door
I dream that I'm back in the traps.
I don't see the confining garden wall,
But the sweep and curve of the track.

And when we go out for our daily walks,
And I move at a stately pace,
My mind tends to wander far away
And I'm back at the front of the race.

On my neck I feel my opponent's breath,
While mine swells strong in my ribs.
Applause, excitement and furious speed
Are a young dog's reason to live.

But now age has caught me, held fast in its grasp,
And I doze many hours away.
Content in my new life, but ready to dream
Of a time when this dog had its day.

Merilyn Hill

A Tribute To My Dog Rosie

(Who is one month from her 20th birthday as I write, June 2010.)

When she is gone my shadow will have left me.
I will have lost a limb. Or a shoe without which
I cannot walk. I will have only one eye, one ear
and will carry with me an empty space that will

forever be Rosie-shaped. There will be no more
one-sided conversations or quiet company when
I am in need. No interpretation of her language
and the pleasure of buying her treats. No one

will come looking when I leave the room.
Or wait behind the door for me to enter.
I shall watch TV or read without her presence
and will not feel the need for all-weather walks.

Yet my heart shall hold her always.
For she embedded herself within me so very long ago
and when I remember, she will be there.
Shining with the love and loyalty she gave so freely.

Miki Byrne

Little Lion

Prowling around the streets at night,
not feeling a single ounce of fright.
For when the darkness sweeps around,
the time is right, his energy found.

His eyes reflecting off the moon,
he must return to his home soon.
His soft paws padding down the lane,
he swishes his tail, smoothes his mane.

The people of the village were rather scared,
but to tame this beast, not one person dared.
That was, until at an early hour,
someone appeared who had this power.

Nobody knows how or why,
but that night there was no roar to shake the sky.
Instead, in that fearsome lion's place,
was a small tabby cat with an innocent face.

Instead of roaring, he purred and miaowed
and now he was mine, he made me proud.
To see him every time I awoke,
to know he listened when I spoke.

Though on the outside, he's now a cat,
on the inside, he feels bigger than that.
He's still a lion, king of the jungle,
ever gracious, always humble.

Now this is the cat I love so much,
he can fix anything with his soft warm touch.
A tiny lick from his sandpaper tongue,
here with this little lion is where I belong.

Morgan Rustidge (13)

My Mr Jinks

On my way home one late February morn,
I stopped off to see some orphans not long born.
To my eyes a surprise I came upon, a little male with a hairless tail,
All curled up in his tiny bed, he looked underfed and very frail.

To home we fled and care we shared,
It didn't take long for him to be reared.
My Mr Jinks is like a minx,
Some people call him the royal Irish sphinx.

He's ever so clever and he can smell the weather,
But I'll tell you something he's not tough like leather.
If he gets caught in a shower he cowers under the flowers,
Then expects me, to towel dry him, within the hour.

He's very athletic and fit as a fiddle,
And can twiddle a ball with antics you'd - giggle.
At times he can be very bold -
Like in the garden often he digs holes.

Any intruders he kicks up a stink,
And chases them out, now they will - rethink -
He stands to attention when I take my tea
Out in the garden, he hovers by the tree.

My Mr Jinks is protective of me,
And at night scans - the street, before he retreats.
Then he jumps on the bed and kisses my head,
Then throws himself over on top of the bed.

Now Mr Jinks as you've probably guessed,
Is certainly not, just any old tom cat.
He knows how to care, and is always aware,
That he is very handsome, and a very - rare - cat.

Pepe Dorton-Hamill

This newly-married cuckoo
Looking for a nest
Told the wife he'd peck her one
Much better than the rest

The local woods were crowded
Not what she had in mind
So the cuckoo took to searching
For something more refined

He found a site of dwellings
Above the two mill band
Then looked out for a tree trunk
For his special Palais Grande

At last he thought he'd found one
At the corner of the lane
Found a likely pecking place
For his ill-planned building game

Full of misplaced confidence
Construction work began
His beak just went to nothing
In the failure of his plan

Unwittingly the place chose
To play as nesting host
Was just beneath a lighting arm
Of a solid concrete post

He told his wife about it
And as they often do
She nagged the hapless husband
Till he sought for pastures new.

Ray Ryan

My Kitty Has Six Legs

(An acting-out poem for Grades 2-3)

My Calico has two invisible legs.
They help her hang on to v-e-r-y thin branches,
and climb straight up a brick wall to get the clock.
I know they are there by the way she walks:
front left foot, middle waddle, back right foot,
front right foot, middle waddle, back left foot;
front shoulders showing muscles like a lion,
stomach bouncing back and forth like a basketball,
back end sashaying like a fashion model down a runway.
Her tail is up like a flag, with the top kinked over,
so invisible kittens can find her in the tall grass.
That is how she moves, except when she's pussy-footing:
her body like a bullet propelled by six trotting legs:
'Don't close the door! It's raining out!'
'Let me out! I saw something move!'
'Let me in! It's dinnertime!'
She must have two invisible legs, because when you rub her belly
she stretches our s-o f-a-r, she couldn't possibly
stand up without support in the middle.
When she washes her face, she never tips over:
I think her invisible legs are out,
like spreaders on a backhoe.
When the dog plays with her, something flashes
out of nowhere to scratch the dog and make him cry.
I never saw it. It must be invisible!
There must be six legs because there are far too many scratches on the furniture.
When she finds your toes under the blanket, it feels like at least six sets of claws!
When she catches her prey, it is invisibly
knocked to the ground and held there,
until she figures out where it is.
Yes, I've been watching my kitty,
and I think she has at least six legs!

Ruth Hill

Lady Sophie

Just from the name you might assume,
That yes, my cat is rather posh!

A look of pure disgust upon her face,
Whenever you reach out to stroke her,
Often greeting you with no less than a glare, as though to say, 'Don't touch me!'

Sophie is to be honest, rather independent,
Like most cats are meant to be!
With a walk, more like a strut and a tail held high,
You could be mistaken for thinking she's untouchable!
But behind that cold demeanour
There's a real pussycat inside.

Poor scared Sophie, leapt clean across the living room,
After something menacing spooked her through the window!
Best not to mention the broken blind . . .
Left hanging disfigured and abused.

She has that killer instinct, I'll give her that!
But sadly not the brains,
Unable to remember the location of her food bowl:
'It's not like we move it Sophie, *ever!*'

There are moments though,
Actually, quite frequent moments,
When she shows that maybe, just maybe, she likes us after all . . .
Cheekily stopping right under my feet,
And with a loving glance upwards,
She miaows, flops over and demands,
In a very madam-like way of course:
A stroke, a rub and on the odd occasion, a good old-fashioned cuddle.

Though one word of warning about our Lady Sophie,
One moment she's purring,
The next, she thinks your arm's a mouse. Ouch!

Sarah George

Our Cat Mo

Youngest of the litter
Lying down, snuggled up with his mum
Sniffing the air all around him
Candy, his mum, moved her litter to a safer place
Sucking his mother's milk
Soft and silky
Fluffy as a ball
Leaping and jumping all around
Very scatty
Now he sleeps stretching out
Loving and caring

Sarah Frances Langridge

Bicardi Cat

Bicardi is nine years old,
We've had him since a kitten,
As soon as we saw his little face,
All of us were smitten.

He's grown so tall and handsome,
He's also very fit.
We think if he was human,
He would be Brad Pitt.

He has a friend who visits,
Every single day
Bicardi waits for him to eat
Then they both go out to play.

Together they chase birds
And try to catch some mice.
They're the best of buddies.
What a super life!

Every night at 6 o'clock
He swaggers down the street.
He goes to visit Auntie
Who gives him lots of treats.

When he's tired and sleepy,
He cuddles me real tight.
He purrs and purrs
And sounds just like a little motorbike.

To us he is so special,
A little lion king.
We wouldn't change him for the world,
Not for anything!

Joyce Cuthbertson

Crazy Frog Poem

Ding-ding
And we start another day

Ding-dong
And that frog won't go away

Ding-ding
So you left me to myself

Ding-dong
And then you offered help

Ding-ding
And he might even have another

Ding-dong
And now Kermy has a brother

Ding-ding
And you know it won't be long

Ding-dong
Before that frog gets number 1.

Anthony O'Regan

My Cats!

My cats are completely crazy
They're always on the go
When I hear a crash in the kitchen
I always think, *oh no!*

When claws sink into bare feet
And I let out a terrible yell
I see one running up the stairs
Just like a bat out of hell

I hear them growling and snarling
Competing to sit on my knee
Can't they just be nice to each other
And accept they have to share me?

My curtains have all got big holes in
My sofa's all bitten and clawed
They even start on the carpet
If they're feeling very bored

One sits on the stairs by the banister
And whenever the children walk past
She lets out a claw and pulls hairs out
If you don't walk very fast

They rip open the bin bags at midnight
You'd think they were never fed
And to think all they do is stuff their face
Then climb up onto my bed

But for all their trouble, they're family
I'd never be without even one
I need reminding now and then though
Now just look at what they've done!

Stormy Raincloud

A Man's Best Friend

We take you away in devastating state,
We try and help,
But just don't realise,
If you could speak,
Instead of bark.

We would hear you and let you see,
Why don't you feel for your family?
When you were born did you see them?
Or were you deserted in the dark gloomy den?

I heard you were a man's best friend,
I must have heard wrong.
People buy you and then they sell you,
Or even let you starve to death,
Why?
I don't even know,
If I could help I would show,
Show the world who is the foe!

People believe,
A man's best friend,
Is real and functional at birth,
And as he ages,
He becomes redundant,
And surprisingly invisible,
But if he was worth a grand,
Then they would understand.

Nassim Ahmed (14)

Gone Too Soon

It seems no time at all since when
You brought them home with you,
You trained them, cherished them and then
You watched them as they grew.

You thought you had a lifetime long,
To live and love and play,
And suddenly it feels so wrong
That they've been snatched away.

Those few short days were all you had,
The angels called too soon,
The hope, the joy seem now so sad,
A snapshot, flower-strewn.

What happened to those happy years,
The summers in the sun?
All washed away in grief and tears,
Before they had begun.

There must have been a purpose here,
Although you've had to part,
And you will keep your memories near,
As solace for your heart.

Brenda Maple

Gibbs The Cat

That Gibbs the cat he lay all night out on a window ledge.
With legs tucked in and tail wrapped round, he blinked occasionally.
One eye was shut, the other not, to watch the night go by.
Some ants were marching, so exhausting, to master a mouldy crust.
A wheeling bat went screaming past. The fox crept slyly slow.
The hedgehog three rolled up to see but trundled off again.
A slimy slug, Gibbs shuddered, blinked. Just then a mouse appeared,
In stops and starts and pregnant darts, with oh so little time.
A glance above, a pause, a sniff for the silence of the owl.
Magician's cape with headlamp eyes, death floats upon the wind.

Grey sky streaked black and red, Gibbs stirred upon the dawn,
A spider here, a beetle there, 'Quick, hurry from the birds.'
The milk float moan, a barking dog, the postman's tuneless feet.
Jumping down, right on time, at the opening of the door.
Tail erect, a throaty purr to lean between the legs.
Rotating tin of jellied fish, fresh icy, creamy milk.
Body wash with paws and tongue, 'Must find that flaming flea.'
Hide a while in washing pile 'til that lot go to school.
To try this place and test that one to find the nicest spot.
Here it is at last, at last, somewhere to curl up warm.

That Gibbs the cat he lay all day inside a window ledge.
With legs tucked in and tail wrapped round, he blinked occasionally.
One eye was shut, the other not, to watch the day go by.
A restless day of dusty sun, being bothered by a fly.

David Jones

We Named You Sid

You came into our lives by sheer chance,
Or maybe fate, responsible for your descent,
Spinning your web you wrangled into our hearts,
Catching your prey like a predator fighting for survival,
With your web of deceit that traps everything in sight.

At first you were a threat, just a mere creepy-crawly,
But you fascinated us by your mesmerising colours,
Browns, yellows and even hints of green,
Your every movement makes us fall ever so deeper,
Your strength inspiring, gives us hope to succeed.

Fighting for your survival you live each and every day,
Habitual, reliable, loyal to your home,
Out in the open, but close to our hearts,
Independent to us, but safe with us,
Not even the rain can wash you away.

Stephen Richardson

In Tranquillity

(To Mum and Dad with love Edmund.)

In tranquillity, the black raven
And the grey pigeon, on their banquet
Of grass, in Olton, Acocks Green;
A sleepy village of Warwickshire,
Feed on the many courses of insects
Laid before them, laid before them:
In tranquillity, the black raven
And the grey pigeon, on their banquet.

Edmund Saint George Mooney

My Pretty Black Puss

She a bundle of black velvet
Her eyes are of sparkling gold
She's eighteen years old now
For a cat that is quite old!

She only has three legs
She lost one years ago
But I don't think she's missed it
Cos she coped so well you know!

She likes a lot of attention
Indeed she loves a fuss
She's loved by everyone
She's such a pretty puss.

Theresa Hartley-Mace

Old Dog Becky

(To be sung to 'Old MacDonald Had A Farm'.)

Old dog Becky had a walk
        ee I ee I o
and on that walk she sniffed the news
        ee I ee I o
with a sniff, sniff here
and a sniff, sniff there,
here a sniff,
there a sniff,
everywhere a sniff, sniff,
Old dog Becky had a walk,
        ee I ee I o.

Old dog Becky met some dogs,
        ee I ee I o
And all those dogs were dogs she knew,
        ee I ee I o
with a sniff, sniff here
and a sniff, sniff ... where?
here a sniff,
there a sniff,
everywhere a sniff, sniff,
Old dog Becky met some dogs
        ee I ee I o.

Old dog Becky did her stuff
        ee I ee I o
Her old man must pick it up,
        ee I ee I o
with a plop, plop here
and a plop, plop there,
here a plop,
there a plop,
everywhere a plop, plop,
Old dog Becky did her stuff
        ee I ee I ugh!

Old dog Becky went to sleep
        ee I ee I o
and in that sleep she had some dreams
        ee I ee I o
with a twitch, twitch here

and a twitch, twitch there,
here a twitch,
there a twitch,
everywhere a twitch, twitch,
Old dog Becky went to sleep,
ee I ee I o.

Leslie Scrase

Keepsake

'The hairs

She forgot to collect -
Are left behind -
Under every floorboard,
Every beam,
Every clint to the wood's grike.

Her earthly form dissipates:
(We are) reluctant
To clean the house she ran,
To clear away the resonant
Traces she once trod;

It remained so, until Transience sent
His messenger down - on a zephyr -
To ease (our) sorrow,
To relieve her silent, sensitive spirit;
To wash away (all of this) woe.

The last sun that saw (us and) her -
As every follicle ceremonially stirred -
Was a familiar shape stopping short
(As if to savour a precious memory)
Before the threshold she knows.

As if the wind had breath still,
Fighting tooth and claw for heart
And home; clear eyes see (us) before
She resigned to soar ... to leave (us) -
Then and now - to live out (our) lives . . .

And the rest of her own.'

Alexander Cole

Tilly The Pirate Cat

One squinty eye, a furry face,
Blinked at me from the ad they placed.
Home required but make if fast,
This pretty girl's sure not to last.

Do you have the love she needs?
This little ad did plant the seed.
The kids were keen to own a pet,
But I had to get past my husband yet.

My husband shook his head and said,
'She's definitely not sleeping on the bed.
Look at that hair, all long and flowing,
My nose will be sore from all the blowing.

My watering eyes and itchy face,
I'll cough and splutter all over the place,
No medicine can put it right,
I'll sneeze and sneeze almost every night.

Just look how fat she is,' he said,
'A furry basketball with a tiny cat head.
Her legs must rub together and chafe,
No food in the house will ever be safe.

She probably has heart problems to boot,
Just think of the vet bills, that money, that loot!
Let's leave her there, she'll find an owner,
I don't see why we're the financial donor.'

But the kids played dirty, they looked so sad,
They knew they could wear down their dad.
They sobbed, they whinged, they cried to win,
Eventually, he just gave in.

We picked her up and brought her home,
She no longer had to stray and roam.
Yes, she was fat, gigantic, immense,
We could slim her down using common sense.

We fed her less and weighed her food
This put Tilly in a cranky mood.
She bided her time, waiting for her chance,
Leading us on a merry dance.

We thought we had won and she'd lost weight,
But we were fooled, we took the bait.
Tilly whinged at the door, mewing with great zeal,

Over the fence, the neighbour's cat's food to steal.
Tilly is plump, Oh yes, that's true,
But all of us pay her, her due.
She is part of the family, she rules the roost,
And her waistline only slightly reduced.

Slugs of fur upon the floor,
Scratches up my kitchen door.
Sloppy fur balls squelch through toes,
The kitty litter's on the nose.

Tilly the pirate, one-eyed cat,
Is the boss of the house, there's no denying that.
To her tenacity I tip my cap,
Her favourite spot ... my husband's lap.

Gillian Cowley-Grimmond

Rascal

Stray mongrel, lame as a three-legged table,
fur like crepe,
cords of malnutrition stringing his legs,
our five-year-old daughter shepherded in
this Viking ransacker
and we, entangled elsewhere, hadn't energy
or time to damp his licking
so let him stay.

Seventeen years our guest,
he raced the lawn to mud,
punctured the flowerbed,
tunnelled the hedge, chased cats,
wagged pride at all harsh words,
far more at home than we who've always lived here,
more missed than any manor-owning lord.

George Horsman

Dumb - Who Me?

Oh beautiful, dumb pheasant
you make my sad heart sing
when I see you strutting proudly
on the cold October ling.

Oh beautiful, dumb pheasant
with your brightly wattled eye,
do you have to *run* for cover?
Don't you know that you can *fly?*

Oh beautiful, dumb pheasant,
you crowing, strident male,
with your harem round about you
and your long and pointed tail.

Oh beautiful, dumb pheasant,
as you dither in the lane,
as you whirr and flap and cross my path
and scuttle back again!

Oh beautiful, dumb pheasant
in your scarlet, green and brown,
there's only one more dumb than you
- the one who guns you down!

Peter Davies

Dolphin Dance

I love the way the dolphins jump,
twirling around on the tips of their tails,
dancing around my imagination,
their gliding movements never fail,
slicing through water like silver arrows,
cutting through sea like a glittering knife,
leaping and jumping through the shallows,
I have wished to be with them for all of my life.

Now they are leaping, jumping, diving,
terribly close to the harbour wall,
and there I am on a tall, grey rock,
staring amazed and watching it all.

Emilie Sophia Challinor (8)

Milly

Milly, Milly please don't cry
Because the night has not passed by
Please don't wake me from my slumber deep
Because I need my beauty sleep
When I awake you can have a wee
So just for once, please think of me
When I wake up that's how I stay
But you can sleep ten times a day
So Milly, Milly please don't cry
And rest in bed 'til dawn is nigh

Milly, Milly please don't bite,
You charge at me with all your might
You chew my fingers and my toes
And jump up high to reach my nose
The furniture tastes so good to you
That all you want to do is chew
My plants, rugs and slippers have all gone
You've got to learn, you can't keep on
So Milly, Milly please don't bite
I love you, I don't want to fight!

Milly, Milly you're only a baby
You will get better - or is that a maybe?
When you think it's time, you demand your dinner
And in challenging me, you're always the winner
You sit, you stay, you play and walk
What would you say if you could talk?
But you make us laugh, you're such good fun
And as puppies go, you're a special one
And Milly, Milly, you're only a baby
All too soon you'll be a big doggy lady!

Linda Roxburgh

Willis The Guide Dog

Five beautiful little puppies
With coats as black as night
Born into the guide dog family
Helping humans with little or no sight

One little boy stood out from the rest
Different from his sisters and brother
But his mummy knew he was special
With love she wanted him to smother

She wanted to prepare him
Show him wrong from right
He snuggled and cuddled up into her
Looking up into her face with eyes so bright

All too soon the time had come
His mummy's heart was breaking
But way down deep in her heart of hearts
She knew Willis was a fine guide dog in the making

He ran to his mummy for one last hug
She said, 'You stand out from the crowd
Do what you're told and learn a lot
You make your mummy proud'

One last nudge of her gentle head
And Willis was on his way
But she knew he had the potential
To be able to help someone some day

So Willis was brought to Ardrossan
His new home was close to the beach
Surrounded by people who loved him
Life was truly a peach

Just one look and you'd fall in love
Stare into his lovely dark eyes
When he jumps up for a kiss and a cuddle
You really feel you've won a prize

Sometimes he comes to see us
We treasure every visit
He gets endless love and attention
And his favourite treat of tea biscuit

He likes a little coffee
Served in his silver dish
There're lots of other treats he loves

Like chicken and tuna fish!
He'll stay for a year to learn new things
Like buses, shops and trains
He has to learn to 'socialise'
He's so clever with lots of brains

After a year he moves on to Forfar
Harder training and lots of new rules
But he's more than able for all that's involved
At guide dogs' 'big puppy school'

When the training's all done and he's worked so hard
He's put in all those training hours
The trials and tests all sailed through
He's passed with flying colours

Then it's time for him to be matched up
To someone with impaired sight
He'll work with that person for eight years
So the partnership must be just right

He's learnt so many new things
And he's achieved all that he vowed
That day he left his mummy
Because she's very, very proud!

Paula Marion Rankin Jackson

The Cat And The Dog: Two Haikus

The cat

Dyed with the dark night
Your black pupils can see through
The sunlight's secrets

The dog

Although newly grown
Your teeth strong enough to chew
All the hardest days

Changming Yuan

Rosie's Repose

(RIP Rosie, December 1995-August 2010)

Where watery depths greet the welcoming land
Paw prints extend across shimmering sand.
Small shells and seaweed in rock pools remain
The soggy delights in this doggy domain.
A flurry of fur and a bounding ball
Beneath whispering wings of gulls as they call.
On the beckoning beach the chase has begun,
Rosie rejoices in freedom and fun.

Pale autumn sun bathes a warm wooden floor,
The flick of an ear, the twitch of a paw.
Corn-coloured cushions on cream cotton throws,
Black and white fur round a black and wet nose.
Wispy white clouds in a breezy blue sky,
The hint of a glint in a soft chestnut eye.
Bronzed trees in glory, the sun in the west,
Rosie's repose - a companion at rest.

Tara NíBhroin Byrne

The Stray

You sit on my lap,
You lie on my bed,
You're always there when I get home,
But you're wild at heart.
You eat the food I give to you,
But you'd rather catch your own
Because you're wild at heart.
You sleep beside my roaring fire,
Content in its warmth and comfort,
But you're wild at heart.
Do you stay because I want you to?
Or because you choose to?
You make me feel you are mine,
But truly I am yours,
Because you're wild at heart.

Margaret Day

The Cat

Silly cat
Lying there
Tongue hanging out.
Fluffy, furry ball
Of fun and indulgence.
Scratch, scratch, yawn
Move from side to side
What shall I do today?
Eat, sleep, sniff the air.
It is cold.
Chase another cat
Invading my territory!
Eat, sleep, sit
On each lap in turn.
Purr loudly
They like that
It makes them
Want to stroke me more.
Life is good.
A cat's life for me.
I'll come back as a cat.

Ornella Bushell

Poem Cat

Like velvet syrup cat pours down
from the shelf. A delicate paw
ruffling feathers of water silk.
A poem wrote this cat; dipping its

self in the warm cream of her fur
painting delicate whiskers on
a half-seen face. Poem Cat concerns
herself with the universe, she

tiptoes across the keyboard to
a meeting of great minds, leaving
a dream of cornflower eyes in
jumbles of consonants and vowels.

Sue Hardy-Dawson

Rat Matters: Finnegan's Psalm

Our dear Siamese rat entered our lives almost four years before
He came to us from next to the reptile area in a tawdry pet store

We marvelled at his silky beige coat and 'chocolate point' bottom and nose
There and then, we vowed to rescue him from slithering, murderous foes

When handled, he showed a gentle mood; he nuzzled us, *bruxed* and soon *boggled*
That his sentient kind are sold as snake food sucks ... we felto so damn boondoggled

(The tooth grind, or *brux*, signifies peace; a *boggle* is
when pet rats' eyes *pop-pop* in ecstasy)
Whiskers twitched on his cute face - complete with crimson eyes that couldn't much see . . .

Finnegan's health began to fade but his playful character and clever mind were still bright
There was a lull in his energy (though his age was a
factor) but he had not lost the will to fight

The scariest of diseases ran full-power, and pain grew insistent for our best furry friend
Yet, he showered our hands in kisses to show he was in no hurry for the love-fest to end

We took him to the veterinarian, so he could get the best prescribed sedation
We fed him 'gourmet vegetarian', in which we put some liquid medication

The vet suggested Finnegan be 'put down' to spare *us* the ugliness of his mouth cancer
She said, 'He'll love you on The Other Side' - (like that vet was akin to a necromancer)

We hoped Finn would pass away at home, and we wanted his ... shift ... to be pleasant
Surrounded by his bub (pet rat) and human family (because it's a gift to be present)

We were moved by just how spirited our elderly 'fuzzy-butt' did remain
Though we worried that rogue cells would quickly strut towards his brain

When we looked at his twisted lips in such a horrid mess
How long he'd be with us had become a fairy easy guess

To those who brayed, 'He's *just a rat*' - hey, ' ... *just a cat*
... just a dog ... ' - all same-sized souls
Finnegan's life mattered - as did our love for him - that
he has gone has left us shot full of holes

Stung and hurt, I nevertheless tried to stay strong so as
to comfort the brave rat kin in my palm

Balm for my heart - as we flung dirt on his tea tin coffin;
was that this was wee Finnegan's psalm.

SheLa Nefertiti Morrison

Untitled

I awoke with a start as if from a terrible fright
I didn't feel rested, mustn't have slept through the night
I was trapped in the bed, held down by the cover
It was then I was aware, of one, then the other

With their job carried out it was time to get up
They bounced over my body as if they were kitten and pup
Strange though it seems they are sweetness and light
But only at bedtime as normally they'd fight

They both had their time, their place and routines
I was just the portal for feeding their needs
They would keep their distance and stick to their sides
With one in the living room, the other upstairs

Hide-and-seek was a game that the cat used to play
But the dog knew her tricks, at my feet he would stay
She would lie in wait for him, always ready to pounce
He would try to run past her, as quick as a mouse

Then evening would arrive and the last walk of the night
Down the road we would go with the cat following in flight
In the long grass on the field they would sniff and give chase
Then back to our house to settle in a warm place

The days would go on with a similar routine
With me running round just to keep the place clean
In the day they were enemies with territories to claim
At night they were best friends, together they would lay
Then the day we all dread, for each to depart
First the dog, then the cat, my best friends leave a hole in my heart

Yvonne Michelle Humphries

Barker

Bark, bark, bark,
All he does is bark,
In the house,
In the car,
And also on the park.

Yap, yap, yap,
He loves to have a yap,
It's all Sam does,
It's in his nature,
From the Watford Gap right off the map.

Howl, howl, howl,
At night he loves to howl,
Whenever we go out,
Whenever he's on his own,
He could do it for England heart and soul.

Jonathan Simms

Fifi The Singing Pussy

It was early in the morning
when the sun came up the street
making Fifi stretch her paws out
when it warmed her furry feet

All the birds were in the trees
singing out their morning song
and it made my cat feel happy
so she planned to sing along

Well she started very softly
till she practised quite a few
but the neighbours didn't like to hear
this pussycat's miaow

Stones and bricks and boots and shoes
they threw with all their might
till the pussy with a last miaow
reluctantly took flight

'Well it seems to me,' the pussy said
'if birds can chirp and tweet
then a miaow from a pussycat
is every bit as sweet

Perhaps with much more practice
I could even learn to cheep
then I'll try it out again
when I think they're fast asleep.'

Evelyn Roxburgh

Georgie Is Cold

Eight years old
the little girl skips
to the garden
to feed the rabbit.
'Georgie is cold!'
Her heart grows old,
she learns of death
and the stopping of breath
and heat.
The little rabbit's feet
are ugly now
and frightening to
behold.
Not in Heaven
but buried under soil
I saw you lift him with the
spade.
It looked undignified
soft fur (enclosed)
in mud,
and then you patted it down
like you would a pet
and thought I would
forget.

In vintage shops
little rabbit feet once used for dusting, dainty women
hang.
They sway like leaves.

Paw prints on cheeks,
the blood has turned to pink powder.

Charise Clarke

Aslan

I had a dog called Aslan
I loved him to the end
He was so golden and cuddly
And such a special friend.

He loved to go a-walking
And swimming in the sea
Then come out of the water
And shake it over me.

Sometimes he would sit
Sometimes he would run
Sometimes he would be playful
And we would have great fun.

Freya Graham (10)

Dusty

The only animal I have really loved
Was an old English sheepdog we called Dusty.
I have never really loved another.
Now he is dead I don't want to experience that pain again.
I like people rather than animals.
At least they can talk.
But there are people I would rather be rid of - without.
People can be much more of a nuisance than animals.
Animals just love you because you provide a home for them and food for them.
Dogs love you for the interesting walks.
They could just as easily love someone else for the same reasons.
How like people they really are!

Sheila Bruce

Sam's Soliloquy

I'm Sam. I'm a black Labrador,
But I'm not chasing cats anymore.
For one of my legs has broken bones
And my head is ensconced in one of those 'cones'.
It seems right now I'm off to the vet.
Though I am not a pampered pet.
Out on a shoot is where I belong
And soon I'll be there - I am strong.
My master really must have arms of steel
When he scoops me up - he keeps an even keel.
I will repay him with each pheasant that falls
And stay by his side through sunshine - and squalls!
Now Meg and Jim too - along with me,
Follow him ever devotedly.

Beryl Mapperley

Beauty Hunting Queen

Your claws catch on a branch
As you lead the bird
On a merry dance
From one branch to another
You go to and fro
Then jump to another tree
But the bird flies away from thee
You're so fast I see
So fast and so free
You love to climb up a tree
To chase the birds is so much fun
As you run in the sun
Now it's mice that you chase
The field is your chosen place
You leave them in a daze
You're so quick in the haze
A jump and you're in first place
Lucky with your first blow

You bring the mouse to the door
So I can count the score
Tomorrow you will catch more
And put them on the floor.

Gordon Forbes

Gauguin's Dogs

We walk the halls of Gauguin's works,
Wonder at his saturated colour, exotic lands,
Soft pink beaches and turquoise seas,
Golden women tinged with umber and rose,
Lilac shadows and lush bright trees.
Then I realise I have been spotting dogs,
Dogs underfoot in every monumental work;
Just your basic merry dog, brown and thin,
Paws splayed and tail at a curious droop,
Dogs quite content with their niche in life,
Running with the skinny island horses,
Standing cocky in the midst of crowds,
The dog that no one ever quite knows
Whose dog he is, but throws scraps anyway.
No one ever strokes that harsh brown fur
Which glints in sunshine, just thick enough
To keep him warm at night. He has
Ears at a jaunty angle, catching voices,
Eyes a berry-brown, watchful and bright.
I have met these dogs on island days,
These dogs who will walk a while with you,
Enriching you with undemanding company,
These dogs who will survive on their wits,
Fading into gaunt old age, and I wonder,
Did Gauguin just put them in to fill a space,
Or like a canine Doctor Who, did they push through
The interstices of his works just to nose around,
And now are trapped for all time?

Liz Davies

Peanut And Socks

My two cats: Peanut is a ginger tom
And Socks is a black tom with white paws
Anyway as I entered my kitchen, at the corner of my eye
Is the rubbish bin all over the floor
'Oh no,' I scream, the two cats run through the cat flap.

They both run through the broken gate
And down by the old farmyard
Past the windmill and up to the old barn where it's full of hay.

Suddenly a ladder reaching to the attic falls
And startles the two cats
They run and hide under an old cart wheel
Peace at last, then suddenly Peanut spots a mouse
He pounces and Socks follows
The mouse luckily escapes
Poor Peanut and Socks are both tired and hungry
Pop their heads through the cat flap
And slowly slumber in, quietly they sit on their mat
'Well there you both are, I suppose you're both tired and hungry.
How would your favourite fresh salmon do
Because all said and done I do love you.'
Happily both are purring around my legs
'I forgive you if you forgive me frightening you both.'

Debbie Storey

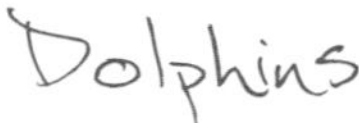

When sailing the uncharted seas,
Man needs a friend, and it's plain to see
The silver fin,
The glossy skin,
The dolphin, it moves slowly in
The deep blue sea, so wild and free,
The dolphin swims so naturally.
The eyes that see,
Oh, what they see,
The dolphin, it inspires me.

The ice-cold sea it doesn't mind,
Instead it tends to spend the time
Rolling, playing,
Bouncing, delaying the ever-moving sea.
The dolphin it plays along with me.

I love the dolphin.

Chloe Howard (12)

Four Legs Good, Two Legs Bad

You listen, but don't reply
You follow, but seldom lead

You eat, and never retaliate
You howl, but never cry

You lay at my feet
But never take the ground from beneath me

You protect me all through the night
While I render you to the elements of nature

You run to the gate to greet me
Whilst I walk past you in my frustration

You want to be on the clouds of freedom
Whilst I chain you to a cage

I buy you to own you
You love me for free

I say that I am your owner
But I pick up your droppings

I wonder at times
If I am the owner, or you are

I realise that two legs are bad, and four legs are good
That four legs are good, and two legs are bad

Shiksha Dheda

My Cat Treacle

My cat's really small and very sweet,
He has a small head and really small feet
He walks by me, rubs his head on my knee,
I don't know what he wants me to see
And when I come home he's waiting for me.
I run up the garden, he chases me!
I've had my cat since he was three
He means everything in the world to me.

Marion Dines

My Cat Treacle

My cat's really small and very sweet,
He has a small head and really small feet
He walks by me, rubs his head on my knee,
I don't know what he wants me to see
And when I come home he's waiting for me.
I run up the garden, he chases me!
I've had my cat since he was three
He means everything in the world to me.

Marion Dines

Bollo (Beagle)

Flapping fur ears and scratchy feet,
peak on belly and tapered tail
follows me down rainy street;
glazed chestnuts looking skywards.

Padding steps stop!
Bold pouty howl emits
from glistening meaty chops.

Black nose powers
a curious sniff.
A hell-bent scent he must devour.

Head tilts and ears bounce,
eyebrows frown
creased in carnivorous concentration.

Lead extends backwards;
Sticky pavement gum fixation.

Tamaragh Docherty

My Best Friend

His two different coloured tail,
Sways in the wind,
It is always up,
For his happiness never ends,

Combined with colours,
Every inch,
Hair falls perfectly,
In line for he is so divine,

Wetness covers you,
As he tells you he loves,
With all his might,
You cannot say no to those chocolate eyes,

He never goes sad,
Above all this,
His bounce tells,
That there is love in him,

He is my cosy blanket,
I never let go,
For you are to know,
He is our charm,

Like a graceful swan,
Gliding through the water he will never leave,
Similar to a gorilla he will stand his ground,
But his love is everlasting.

Abbey Varns (10)

What She Didn't Say

She did say he was 'spirited'
As adoption papers signed
We took Kenny from Cat Rescue home,
Only there to find

He was in fact completely mad
A total mental midget
Unhinged, deranged, devoid of brain
And here is how he proved it

From deepest slumber on a lap
He'd leap into the air
Body arched, squirrel tailed
He'd dive under a chair

With pupils sized to organ stops
He'd launch, a blackened blur
Sink his teeth into your toe
Then leave you with a purr

He'd lie in wait, in the hall
Black in black, raised hackles
Wait till human climbs the stair
Then trip with rugby tackles

Or better yet to eyes unseen
Lurk on darkened landing
Then strike through spindled banister
And seldom leave you standing

He threaded sofas, swung from voile
Bought pheasants in the house
Upset bins, ate the plants
Invited home a mouse

For ease we opted for a cat
Less hassle than a dog
Because you hardly know it's there
Not so our mad black mog

But other things, she didn't say
At least I don't recall
Were how much fun would come
With this feline cannonball

How every time we came home
He'd be at the gate waiting
To smother us with honest love
No food anticipating
How every time we sit down
We have to be as three
Myself, my son and
Of course, devoted cat on knee

How our home, now ripped to shreds
By fearsome feline claw
Is richer for the presence of
A pet we both adore.

Sarah Dukes

A Man's Best Friend

A man's best friend, that's what they say
As a dog, I don't see it that way.
Women have done so much more,
It's Olivia my owner, I really adore.

She is always there whenever I need her,
She's like a sister, she's like a leader.
We're very alike, personality I mean,
Doing our best to be heard and seen.

Our friendship is like a chemical bond,
It can't be broken, unless something's gone wrong.
She sneaks me treats, she sneaks me food
She tells me off when I am rude.

Although I may get in the way
Well that's what the rest of the family say,
But gentle Olivia just strokes my side
What a lovely girl, so sweet and kind.

My poem is almost over now,
But there is one more thing I must say,
Olivia, I love you
In every single way.

Flora xxx

Olivia Buckley (12)

Skye

I call her name
and gracefully, elegantly she bounds up to me.

Ever obedient she waits for the meaty treat
and devours it silently.

Her big brown eyes bore me for yet another treat
but I shake my head and solemnly she wanders away.

Locked in her own private world
she searches and sniffs for anything edible.

Ever curious she gnaws at wood
her collar tinkles as she bites

She is playful, mischievous and a little devil
but she's my little pup and I love her to bits.

Hannah Hamilton (11)

Cheeky's Revenge

A project was happening - a house renovation,
And our family was stressed with but one reservation.
Not the price, nor the mess, no nothing like that,
Instead we were stressed about Cheeky the cat.
Cheeky was clever, Cheeky was shrewd,
And sometimes he bordered on being quite rude.
A house full of builders would give him great joy,
He'd torment and tease, every trick he'd employ.
So the laundry became Cheeky's place to reside,
The rest of the house, he was firmly denied.
We explained to the builders he must not be let out,
That he'd cause endless trouble when wandering about.
Well the builders they smirked and nodded their heads,
Somewhat amused by what we had said.
So our family stayed watchful from morning 'til night,
With Cheeky the cat kept well within sight.
But, as is often the case with a run of good luck,
On the last day of building, our plan came unstuck.
As the tiler cemented the final floor tile,
And varnish on floors had been drying a while,
We discovered the laundry empty and bare,
Cheeky the cat was no longer there.
The tradesmen all grinned and packed up their gear,
Our plea of 'please help us', just fell on deaf ears.
We searched all the bedrooms, the lounge and the hall,
But Cheeky was gone - he was nowhere at all.
'We'll just have to wait,' my tired mother said.
'Let's hope he comes home when he needs to be fed.'
It was later that night when from under the floor,
Came a tortured miaow - it was Cheeky for sure.
We stood on the tiles, staring down at our feet,
Unable to fathom, the cat trapped underneath.
'Well this is a hassle,' my mother announced,
As out to the shed she went with a flounce.
She returned with the axe and before we could speak,
Chopped into a floorboard of beautiful teak.
Quick as a flash, Cheeky leapt through the hole,
And casually sauntered across to his bowl.
As he chomped his way through his ocean-fresh fish,
We all stared at the floorboards, now shattered in bits.
It was then that the builder decided to ring,
To inform us that he had forgotten one thing.

'The floorboard,' he said, 'at the end of the hall,
Isn't nailed down, if it tilts, you could fall.'
'Well,' said my mother, 'I'll see you at eight,
And if I were you, I wouldn't be late.
You have other boards that now need to be fixed,
Because you've been victim of Cheeky's smart tricks.'

Caroline Tuohey

Nocturnal

You begin at midnight when the lights are out,
A soft shuffling at first, like the wearied feet of morning
But backwards.
A scuffle and dance, the drip-drop of water;
The tick-tock of the daunting clock on and on and on.

I lie like an insomniac, flat on my back and watch.
Cautious you test it; the never-ending wheel,
One paw, two paw, three and then four and you're in,
You're running, you're breathless and wild and free without freedom.
An incessant whir of a turn going nowhere

Then *stop!*

I am up now, restless, pacing, we watch each other
In silence, shivering in the cold night, thinking and thinking
The problems of day that have followed us here into this;
The safety of darkness, where safeness is short-lived
And we hope.

Nocturnal creatures of the after-light, we sit;
You on my shoulder, and I on the floor,
Considering our sanctuary, surrounded by sawdust,
Indoors, in our nest, where the light doesn't break us when the sun rises
And we cuddle up, facing the day, warm in our blankets and straw.

Sian Altman

A Dog's Life

We got him at six weeks old
A fluffy ball of fun
He was one of seven pups
We knew he was the one
His little eyes were gleaming
His fur was black and gold
His ears were small and floppy
We saw him and he was sold!

As the little pup got older
His ears and paws looked large
Like a baby police dog
Trying to take charge
He had a cheeky character
Tried to get his own way
Always won me over
Always made me play

Now a German Shepherd in his prime
Handsome and mature
He turned heads wherever he went
A pedigree for sure
He was loving and protective
He'd defend me with his life
He didn't trust just anyone
Senses sharp as a knife

Now he is in his later years
His chin is growing grey
He's slowing down and resting more
He's doing things his way
His poor old legs are failing
On me he does depend
I'll love that dog forever
Sabes, my loving loyal friend.

Tracey Carter

My dog's name is Cassie, she's such a bonny lassie
Some folks may disagree though
Their thoughts means naught to me.
She's full of health, bounce and vigour
With let's just say 'a doggy figure'.
Hair that shines like the dead of night
That's right, you've guessed she isn't white
Eyes that sparkle like morning dew;
Floppy ears and shiny black nose too.
She came to me just a ball of fluff
Even now she's not 'tough stuff'.
She stands beside me, loyal and calm
Keeping me, if need, from harm.
When at times there's just her and me
She'll sneak and sit upon my knee.
If I'm worried or feeling blue
She's the one I tell my secrets too,
For though she has a listening ear
Of them being repeated I have no fear.

Susan Kaye

The Hill

The kingfisher - resplendent in its blue plumage,
Perches on a 'No Fishing' sign near the rippling pond.
A Canada goose sits, huddled on the far bank.
A buzzard glides in the blue sky above, on the wind eddies
Searching with graceful movement for rodents.
Meanwhile you can hear the brook bubbling in the distance
As a deer darts through the trees
Stampeding on the wild primroses.

Matthew Lee

My Beloved Cat Cami

If my beloved cat Cami never died
She would be here
Lapping up fun
Dancing in sunlight

And I would play with her
She who was in
A league of her own

She was quite a gal
Great fun to be with
And I wrote her odes
And we two rode the ride that's life

And I still worry about her
When in my mind
She crouches on a high perch
I never want her to miss a step
Fall and get hurt

However much I try to forget her
She's always there

Muhammad Khurram Salim

Shep The Footballer Sheepdog

Our dog Shep is our family pet,
We've had him for about three years,
Acquired him as a pup,
From a family lacking love,
For a cuddly black and white ball of fluff.

But there's something about Shep that makes him outset,
From all other canines you see,
Give him a football,
And he's surely as sure,
He'll play soccer with his big paddy paws.

Nose pointed to sky and flying high,
Shep headers it up in the air,
When it comes down,
Back onto the ground,
He'll push it for you to kick it again.

If my son's out kicking a ball about,
It drives soccer Shep crazy mad,
With a woof, howl and din,
He'll open the door with his chin,
So he can get out in order to join in.

If out for a walk at the local park,
Shep has to be kept on a leash,
For he'll beg and he'll plead,
To be off his lead,
To the boys playing soccer, he's the goalie they need.

Soccer-mad Shep, our very fit pet,
Footy on his mind all day,
He doesn't want fame,
Just a chance to train,
With Wayne Rooney, that would be his dream.

Lynda Bray

My Poem About My Rabbit

I remember the day I got my rabbit
He had no name so I named him Noddy
There in a pet carrier next to me in the car
So cute and fluffy my little rabbit Noddy
My rabbit Noddy is so cute when he twitches his nose
Hops about the garden and jumps on my toes.
He hides in the bushes and we can't get him out

He eats all his lettuce, *chew, chew*
And he also likes to bite through cables too
But then he stops, my mum cuts his nails
While I make his dinner: carrots, lettuce
And rabbit food then we put him in his hutch
And he goes to sleep

Then in the morning
We wake up then Noddy wakes up
And we give him some breakfast: lettuce and carrots, yum-yum
He gobbles all up then we put him in his run
A while later we let him into the garden
He hides in the bushes
Again my mum struggles to get him out
We take him into the front room
He spots the cable but we grab him just in time
He is so cuddly and soft
I wouldn't trade him for anything in the world
I love my rabbit Noddy

Eloise Shepherd

Doggy In The Oven

(Inspired by Rosie and her friend Lily who always growl at their reflections.)

There's a dog inside our oven,
She often stares at me,
She watches when I eat my food,
And eats the same as me.

There's a dog inside our oven,
She wags her tail a lot,
I hope that she's okay in there,
Sometimes it gets quite hot.

There's a dog inside our oven,
She likes giving me a lick,
But when she hears Mum shouting,
She disappears right quick.

There's a dog inside our oven,
And I really hope one day,
That she'll leave her little oven,
And come outside to play.

Suzanne Rae

My Attitude Cat

My cat has a temperament and a lot of charm
She was found at birth out on a farm
I named her Lucky as she was one of five
Being the only one of her litter to survive
She jumps on my bed early each day
For me to open the door then she is away
She sits in front of my car to stop me going out
And will not move as she is so devout
If she sees me packing a case to go away
She sits on it to try and make me stay
Loves drinking water from the dripping tap
In the right mood she will jump on my lap
Cleans her food dish using her paw
Then looks up as if asking for more
Sundays I feed her tuna for a treat
She knows the day, if no tuna she will not eat
Sits in front of the TV watching the show
When loud music comes on off she will go
Returning home she is there waiting to greet
A more warm and loyal friend I have yet to meet

Leonard A G Butler

Floored Cat

There once was a black and white cat
Who wouldn't sit still on the mat,
He sat on the floor
Right in front of the door
Which when opened would knock him quite flat!

Rachel E Joyce

Ratfink, The Fat, Slobby Cat

Ratfink is tabby, with little white paws,
When she wants to go out, she scratches at doors.
She sits by the heater, in my in-tray,
With her head under the curtain, there she will stay.

She's sitting with one leg up, after scratching her head,
When I'm asleep, she often comes on my bed.
She likes to be tickled under the chin,
It's our little joke that she's not very thin.

My dad gets annoyed, when she scratches at walls,
And like other cats, she never comes when she's called.
When she goes to her tray, it's always something smelly,
A bit like the food she eats to fill her belly.

She's always so lazy; she's hardly ever awake,
Nothing will disturb her, not even an earthquake!
But we all still love her, because she's our cat,
And I know for one there's no better reason than that.

Deborah Coverley (12)

Bracken

(Dedicated to Bracken, who is no longer with us.)

I have a friend who visits me not every day
Just now and then.
I open my door, in he comes,
He sits beside me quietly,
With big brown eyes, looking at me.
He watches and waits patiently,
He knows where I keep his treats.
I would love to have a dog of my own
But it's just not possible,
I'm getting on in years you see,
So I love it when Bracken visits me.
He lives in the big house next door,
He listens to all my tales and woes,
He even gives me his paw.
Then up he gets and toddles off,
He gives a bark to say thank you,
I know he will be back one day soon,
My doggy friend who visits me.

Hazel Storer

Toby's Heaps Of Guts

'That cat never catches a mouse,'
Someone did declare
'All he does is lie around in the house.'
The cat at once did stare
Up he marched towards the door
Swanking his bottom
Tail raised high, he caught my eye
'I'll let him out, I've got him.'

No time at all had passed
Than we heard Toby cry
'Don't say he's back already then
Leave him for a while.'
Bearing in upon our ears
A long drawn-out mowling
We turned to each other, lips a-pursed
What a strange howling
Never heard that before
'Shall I go and look?'
The sound was interspersed with bleats
Is this a kind of flook?

I opened the outer door
I gasped, 'Oh! My goodness!
Guess what boy Toby's done
A mouse he's caught with rudeness.'
Someone said within
'I don't believe it, it's not him.'
'Well come and look.'
They all pile out together.

Disbelief and chortling now scan our canny puss
Clearly someone's exercised his tether
What do you think of that? He glared
My concern is for the victim
'Is he dead now? Well quickly eat him up.'
We all went back inside the house
Don't care to view the munching
Rodents not exactly choice of sup.

Minutes passed and suddenly
Commenced the howling row
You know it's the same tune, louder and how
'That cat again!' Someone's in a pique
'I will go to him,' straight away I speak

As his mistress dear I'll always volunteer
He just does not stop his noise
'Oh! I don't believe it, my!'
I can't hide my surprise
'You really will not credit but
He's caught another mouse.'
Everyone once more piles out the house.

This morsel's wriggling, no hope of escape
Trapped in a jaw like a vice
'Release or, if he's injured, kill!'
Toby does not jape
'All this is down to you.'
Someone is accused
'Our pet you should not criticise
He'd never caught a creature one
He's never had a sniff.'
The animal every stare defies.

He deserves to taste of triumph
But shortly down the line
With us humans each settled in our chair
Came the mowling, yowling
Here we go again!
You can guess what it means
Our hunter must have found some lair.
Checking confirms mouse number three
Four and five duly follow
Seen enough not to the door to go
Someone rings a little hollow.

The night does pass away
And in the morning fair
Behold! The pavement by the porch
Little heaps of guts deposited bare
We counted eight
There is no more to say.
Appearing at the end of day
The cat rounds on us full square:

'Next time you're tempted to have a go
Look to your own laurels
It's not that I've become
A feline without morals
Just promise me I'll hear no more
Of your tiresome quarrels!'

Valerie Jenkins

My Cat Tibby

I had a cat named Tibby,
She liked climbing into the fruit bowl,
She liked veg as well as cat food,
And bits of chocolate also,
She would sleep on top of my bed clothes,
All the night long,
Never running outside to go and play,
Never even leaving my side.
Now, Tibby is gone.
Will I ever get another pet?
It is much simpler to live without animals,
And yet,
It is lonely without my dear Tibby,
Sleeping on the mat,
I tell you that I never had before,
Such an unusual cat.

Peter John Morey

Sea Chase

A galloped sand chase was all that he knew,
As he ran towards strangers who followed them through.
A salty side shake and a toss of his head,
Gave no thought for his mother who had simply said,
'Come back here and away, it's to heel you should be.'
But instead he just ran and swam out to sea.
'I've lost my old mongrel. He swims like a snail.'
'Don't worry he's here with his rudder-like tail,
And he bobs up and down and spits like a whale.'
A whistle once more and back he returns,
His nose at the bow and his tail at the stern,
He smells like the sea, he's just salty and soaked,
The job's done, let's go, this old sea dog's been walked!

Audrey Nelson

A Saddened Cat's Lonely Winter

It had been a long hard day
What with festive visitors coming and going
Nowhere was there somewhere nice and peaceful

Nipper - the black & white male tomcat - felt neglected;
relegated - to the cold - outside in the extended porch

He miaowed at his neighbour's back door
Hoping to be let in
Feeling sorry for himself

He would be welcomed to stay awhile
Share some Company
Listening to the Radio in the background -
Tuned to the first stirring movement of Rachmaninov's
Second Piano Concerto

Sombrely dreaming of 'Tabs' - his feline partner
Anguished because she was no longer there
Wondering whether she could possibly love him in his
declining years
Just as she had once promised with an enigmatic meow
that she always would
When they were both in their prime; - so full of life; - and
blissfully unaware

Alan Ernest

Kelly's True Story

When I was eight months old
I was not very bold
One day, I went for a car ride
And on a major road I wanted to hide

Then the car slowed down
And out I was thrown
My owner drove on, leaving me on my own
I was hurt and thought, *how can I get home?*

Then another car stopped, a lady came to me
And put me in her car, took me to the Blue Cross
At least I had a meal and shelter
Instead of being in a car, driving helter-skelter

I was so frightened, then a lady came and sat with me
She talked to me, somehow I felt safe now
The lady took me for a walk, I thought, *wow!*

Next day she came in a car, with a friend
It took four people to get me in
I thought, *when will it end?*
We went to Felixstowe, what fun
A nice walk, cup of tea and a bun

Then I went back to the Blue Cross
The lady said, 'I will be back soon.'
Then one day, they phoned her at noon
I heard them at Blue Cross, tell her I was sad

Next thing she was there to take me home
Where I met her red setter, waiting at home
We became real good pals, that's for sure
Then she became very ill, was given her final rest

To me Gemma was one of the best
Then my mum took me to Blue Cross
Where I saw my caring boss
He was very pleased, to see how well I was

We were shown Ruby, another lurcher
And she came home with us
I am 10 years old now and had two ops to remove lumps
Ruby is 14 years and going grey

We are lucky to have a home, and loved this way
And live as members of a family
We love our mum and we know she loves us
And thanks to all at the Blue Cross.

Love from Kelly.

Joan Read

Mother Love And Pets

Kitten and Mum; put to sleep when war begun
to save them from the German bomb.

When war was done, a new pet life begun
(with children two). Hamsters and tortoise
rabbits, hedgehogs and others taught us
that all of natural life serves us as pets -
house martins, swallows, birds of many orders
came to our house or its adjoining borders
to rear their young: for twenty years or more:
aunts, uncles, grandparents of many generations
came to us to seek our benefaction.
Spiders, caterpillars, butterflies and bees - pets for us
and we should love them as such
(tho' now and then we may not like them very much).

The lion tamer has a pet; he can ignore
Man's dictum 'Nature red in tooth and claw'
He knows full well that deep within the King of Beasts
there lives the mother-love of lioness
that reared the king through infantness.
No beast, no animals at all would be
except that mother love reared them with motherly gentility.

In later life I lived alone . . .
so Ferdie Fieldmouse came seeking warmth within my house
from icy woods, gardens and frozen foods.
Access he made through cracks, cranny, pipe or hole
where uncertain of this strange environment he took a sentry role
till God-wisdom told him it was safe.
He then began his sideways zigzag race
to snatch his food; and then, according to his mood
he'd scamper back, as straight as any arrow
in hiding place, in crevice narrow; or hunt for more upon the floor.

Often he fed from off my shoe - a bold and friendly thing to do.
When springtime came off he did go, to try his luck with food and foe
in woodland house. Farewell, pet mouse.

Sidney Fisher

Animal Antics

You are brushed, well-fed
And I make sure you don't have a mite
To bite your sensitive pink skin
Pink because the hairs on your coat are white.

The vet took your tooth out
It's been kept because it's yours
To me you haven't any flaws.

An appetite the like of what's never been seen before
Have to watch that because you would just keep on eating more.

Had to learn everything green as grass were I
Only knew little bits but knew you were worth it and how hard I must try.
Oh yes we got there and now you are as happy as can be
We get on well together for all to see.

A good scratch on your neck brings from you a pleasant humph
Then pointing your nose at the side of your bum as if saying
Please scratch there, the other bit's done.

You stand there in ecstasy
That's much better you say
It beats rubbing my itchy spot against the trunk of a tree.

You are looked after with ointments and creams bought by the score
Everything checked and there is water for you galore.
Ouch, did you just give me a nip from those long teeth you have in your jaw?

Got to go now, see you tomorrow then you with your soft velvet nose
My handsome cob with the white feathers on your legs, long white tail and mane
My life with you has benefitted me, has kept me sane
So yes for you there will always be a horse blanket
When the weather does turn and we have the wintry cold rain.

A rescue horse you might be but you mean the world to me.
It was me that was rescued and to you I will always be as grateful as can be.

H Dormand

My Special Friend

My friend never judges me
And also seems to know
Just when I need him beside me . . .
He is there when others go
And my friend never ever tries
To tell me what to do
Though I know that I can rely on him
To be a friend who is true
He never ever says to me . . .
Well, I told you so
He accepts me just the way that I am
And my moods he seems to know
I can tell him all of my secrets
Trusting him is easy you see
I know that he will never tell
He just means the world to me
It's true we will love each other
Until the very end
Yes ... my dog is so special
And I'm proud to call him ... friend

Joyce Hudspith

My Best Pal

(A poem about Licksie my Jack Russell terrier)

Her shiny brown eyes are bigger than her tummy and she'll chase anything,
the rabbits down their holes, the swans in the river and usually me.
Golden brow, white flash on her head,
she is cute but alert, and walks forever, even with me.
Running over hills and head in hollows, her white tail wags,
to greet friends and strangers and of course me.
Wet pink tongue, hangs down from a sharp-toothed mouth
keen to lick everyone, but especially me.

She's my best pal, Licksie.

William Kent (8)

Jinx

I never knew what love was until I looked into those big brown eyes.
She doesn't speak a word but we understand each other so well
From a nudge, a lick, a wag of the tail.
She is my best friend, my baby, my favourite companion,
Can tell her my problems and she listens contentedly,
The one thing in my life that will always be there,
Will never leave me, or bear a grudge, or cause me to despair.
And when the time has come for her to pass I know that when I die
I will be greeted by her wagging tail at the pearly gates of Heaven
Where our friendship will be reunited once more and this time never die.

Samantha Forde

Of A Butterfly

As a caterpillar, my pet, my annual friend,
You wriggled and slithered along the ground,
No legs to be seen, all covered in a furry down,
Slowly, laboriously high into a tree you climbed,
Adhering to a leaf,
Forming a chrysalis out of sight and mind,
The leaf wrapped around you to keep you dry and warm,
As the weeks go by Mother Nature takes turn,
Metamorphosis has begun,

Then when the time is right,
Out of your cocoon you slowly slide,
From the larva awakens, a magnificent butterfly,
Unfolding wings as gossamer as silk,
So thin and fine, adorned with a rainbow of colour,
Pure beauty unto the eye,
Opening your wings to the freedom of the wind,
Fluttering from plant to plant,
For sweet nectars, and leaves abound,
But how can something so graceful,
Be born void of any sound?

You grace our Earth with such beauty,
But alas, not for long,
Whence into the trees you fly yet again,
This time ... a mate by your side,
Onto a leaf your eggs to lay,
Slowly caterpillars thus become,
The life cycle to one of life's beauties,
Has yet again begun . . .
Such is the life of my pet ... and annual friend . . .

Barry Pankhurst

Dear Duke

(Dedicated to my lovable, gentle Airedale, Marmaduke Patrick Prancer who had a pedigree much, much longer than his name!)

You were a star in my book
From the moment you held out your tiny paw
You stole my heart.

Brave, yet gentle, kind, yet comic,
On Saturday your ashes were buried
In the garden where you spent so many happy years.

Alex and Louisa brought flowers after school
To show they, like me, miss you so much.
Rest In Peace, my dear four-legged friend.

Betty Lightfoot

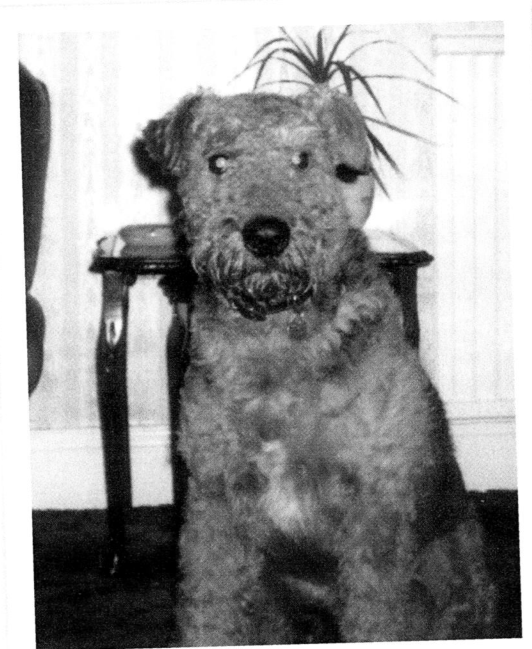

Alpha Dog

We said goodbye to our baby today
We didn't want to, but she couldn't stay.
There's no hairs
On the stairs,
No dish
Oh, how I wish . . .

Somehow it seems worse than for the 'Old Boy'
He too was a character, but with a different ploy.

Is it because she was so quiet and genteel,
She had such appeal?
She was blind, curious and nosy
Couldn't/wouldn't hear, perfect was the coat and nose.

Other dogs revered her, held her in awe
All respected her, it wasn't a chore.
Not aggressive, could be feisty if there was a need,
Independence was her creed.

The house was quiet
Now it's quieter.

But why has it been so hard?
Is it because she rallied?
But she was seventeen she wouldn't ever recover,
Oh bother!

Our alpha dog
Queen of the crop.
There's no tippety toes across the floor
Anymore.

Today it was dull and dreary - and it cried.

Jean Ivatt

Tabitha And Tina

My black and white cats
Waiting patiently
At the kitchen door
Bouncing into
The welcoming warmth
Hoping for some tasty titbit.

My mischievous cats
Catching fat little mice
Proudly presenting them
At my feet
Expecting praise
And some little treat.

My friendly felines
Welcoming me
Each day
As I fill the kettle
For early morning tea
Rubbing up against my legs.

'What is that in your mouth?'
Gently I remove
The frightened sparrow
From my cat's greedy grasp
Releasing it for avid flight
Away from danger and alarm.

My mewing moggies
Eager ears pricking
As I speak
Some welcoming words
Sharp claws protruding
From velvety paws.

My frisky cats
Happily playing
With a favourite toy
Climbing trees
With consummate ease
Resting briefly on a broad branch.

Kate McDonnell

My Little Miracle

Who knew that a tiny eye could see so much?
How can it even see night and day?
How can that tiny dot
See such a lot?
But it does, and that's beyond me.

Who knew that a body could ripple so?
Like waves across a long ocean,
How can such a sea
Only appeal to me?
But it does, and that's beyond me.

Who knew that a mouth of that microscopic size
Could actually make such a sound?
A sort of rasping
Provokes the asking
But it does, and that's beyond me.

Who knew that the brittle shell of a snail
Could actually be beautiful?
A delicate twist
The colours mixed
But it does, and my pet's beyond me!

Megan Naylor (12)

Enclosed A Photo . . .

Enclosed a photo of my cat . . .
She has several names . . .
Now fancy that; favourite of these
Is Butty Boo, cos it rhymes with
How do you do, and I can see you
Also I'm talking to you, Butty Boo.

I sometimes refer to her as Domino
Guess you can tell why? By the photo!
Also with her snow-white bib
My little nun would not sound a fib.
Most of the time we get on fine
And I pet and stroke and call her Sunshine.

When she does something naughty
I smack her and say, 'Butty Boo
This day you will rue!' Then she looks haughty
Leaves the room with docked tail held high
As if to say, 'I'll be back by and by
And because you miss me, you'll hug and kiss me.'

My beauty is there when no one else is
And if I lost her, I'd get into a right tis
Seven years we've been together through thick and thin
And to part with her now would seem like a sin
So together we'll be until the end
Little Butty Boo - my feline friend.

Valerie Hall

Tortoiseshell Bay

(For Dale and Michelle)

She stands on the grass as proud as can be
Watching the sun caress the deep blue sea
Her hooves first attentively touch the soft warm sand
The owner eagerly guiding with sunburnt hand
Her mane and tail sway to the summer breeze
She moves with the grace as a goddess would tease.
Small ripples rush, tapping against her hooves
Gracefully lapping her every move
A chorus of foam sings around her legs
Like the froth building in her mouth as she gently begs
The shiny bit so silvery and cool
Sparkles in the ripples of after pools.
The tide recedes and she's ready to catch
Bold body and long strides are no match
She thunders along the sandy shore
Racing the waves as her eyes hunger for more
Her coat mingles with shingles and sand
As she streaks like lightning along the shore land
She comes to rest at the end of the sun's rays
My goddess!
My beauty!
My tortoiseshell bay.

Linda Gray

We have a very young Great Dane and 'though he's just a pup,
He's big enough to make you think he's really quite grown up.

The other day, when the garden was wet from the rain the night before,
This dog (we call him Danny), made us laugh. He made us roar!

He'd found a paper cup and in his daft and lanky way,
He was bounding around with the cup in his teeth, dropping it, and running away.

Then he'd pick it up again - it all seemed very tame,
Until the cup got stuck on his nose, and this was a different game.

Trying to look at the stuck-on cup and going quite cross-eyed,
He ran around, growling, and madly shaking his head from side to side.

'Oh very amusing Danny!' I laughed as he passed for the second time,
But in blind panic to free himself, he ran through the washing line.

This cross-eyed, cup-nosed muddy dog, wrapped up in shirts and vests
Went hurtling in through the open back door - a whimpering, pitiful mess!

Legs akimbo, Danny skidded across the kitchen floor,
And scrambling frantically, trying to stop, crashing into the larder door.

He lay there in a tangled heap, a really funny sight.
We sorted him out, he slumped onto his blanket - and he didn't move all night.

Bill Eden

A Furry Friend

A furry friend that's there till the end.
Loving from the start.
Right till the last beat of his heart.

His bark's worse than his bite
And you sure will get a fright if he growls through the night.
But you've grown to love him through the years
And his soft fur wipes away your tears.

He's the one thing that's there for you.
The one person you can tell anything to.
Yes, he's better than that silly purring 'mog'.
Yes, I love him cos he's my dog.

Ellie Finnigan (13)

Taca

A tiny bundle of black and white fluff
Yet still with unseeing eyes
So tiny and defenceless
That day you came into our lives

Many days and nights have passed by
Since that memorable day
And you've grown into a canny bitch
So fearless, strong and brave

The rats and mice inhabiting
Our garden live in fear
And never venture out
When they know that you are near

Butterflies and even frogs
Birds and snails and bees
All are at the mercy
Of your canine curiosity

Your agility is astounding
Never ceasing to amaze
Leaping, romping and delving
Obeying your instinctive ways

Let your questioning wet muzzle
Your unexploited heart
Your innocence and devotion
Remain with us till death us do part.

Susan Jacqueline Roberts

What A Lovely Day For A Dip!

What a lovely day for a dip,
such a lovely day for a dip.
I'll wag my tail,
and I'll lick my lip
what a lovely day for a dip!

What a lovely day for a run,
such a lovely day for a run.
I'll fetch my stick
and we'll all have fun
what a lovely day for a run!

What a lovely day for a walk,
such a lovely day for a walk.
I'll stretch my paws
and the ducks will squawk
'What a lovely day for a walk!'

What a lovely day for a dip,
such a lovely day for a dip.
I'll wag my tail
and I'll lick my lip,
and we'll all have fun,
and I'll run, run, run,
and my paws I'll stretch,
and my stick I'll fetch,
and I'll walk, walk, walk,
and the ducks will squawk
'What a lovely day for
a dip,
    a run,
        a walk!'

Sonya McConaghy

Animal Madness

If humans could be animals,
What would they choose?
A giraffe with a scarf,
Or a centipede with shoes?

A leopard with glasses,
Or an elephant with hair?
A hedgehog with an Afro,
Or maybe even a mole that's part bear?

A duck with teeth,
Or half-pony, half-pig?
A toad with fake eyeslashes,
Or even a parrot with a wig?

A turtle that goes moo,
Or a gorilla with a beak?
An octopus with a bikini,
Or even a spider that goes squeak?

So if you could pick
What would you be?
A mouse with a tutu,
Might reflect your personality!

Megan Capaldi-Tallon (12)

Squirrel

Squirrel, she's a funny little thing,
Carries, a bushy tail,
Patters up the garden steps,
And comes in with the mail.

Squirrel, she has velvet fur
Her fur is chestnut brown,
She has big round pleading eyes,
When she wants to be put down!

Squirrel, she's a fearless thing,
Nibbles food in her hand
Loves to eat the nuts and berries
That we put out in her stand.

Squirrel, she's a funny little thing,
Cares about her babies,
Stores some food in her cheeks
And hides them in the trees!

Khadijah Majid (9)

My Cat Yesterday

You wouldn't believe Sid yesterday,
he slept and slept
as it rained and rained,
and when he did want to go out and play
the rain just wouldn't go away.
There he sat by the door,
tail angrily swishing on the floor,
I booted him out,
one minute later he came in again
drenched with water.
I got a towel and gave him a rub
and a plate of his favourite grub,
he lapped it up with a hearty purr
and settled down and licked his fur.
There he gave a mighty yawn
and slept again 'til dawn.

Angie Cotterill

Cedric - My Crocodile

I had a baby crocodile
Of which I was so fond,
I called him Cedric, and I kept
Him in the garden pond.

But he ate up all the tadpoles,
The carp and goldfish too,
And his thrashing and his churning
Turned the pond-mud into stew.

When birds came down to drink and bathe
He'd snap at them and roar,
And very soon no wildlife came
To bathe there anymore.

He would plod around the garden
And dig up all the flowers,
And sun himself upon the lawn
For hours and hours and hours.

Soon no one came to visit us,
The postman failed to call,
The newspapers and milk were left
Out on the garden wall.

With all the love I gave to him
He grew and grew, and so
Mother said that Cedric
Had really better go.

We gave him to the local zoo,
Now he has friends to share
His large wildlife enclosure park,
He's very happy there.

I often go to visit him,
And stay and chat awhile,
I know that he remembers me,
Cedric - my crocodile.

Ann Dempsey

My Yorkie, Terry Thomas

Given this chance I can't let pass
To tell you of my cheeky imp Terry Thomas
He was once mistaken for a mini Highland cow
Until his forced bow wow wow wow wow
If one could see his big black eyes
Might well say they'd win a prize
But my wee pet does not care
About keeping ribbons in his hair
Still loves being told he is a bonnie laddie
Gets well lost if called a baddie
When one asks, 'What's that you've got?'
He defies, growls and prances on the spot
Hides and whimpers, full of wrath
At merest whisper of a bath
Just cannot boast of his grand pedigree
As starts off his capers for all to see
Knows more tricks than tongue can tell
Has a most patient master and just as well
Do pity me in toeless odd slippers
A top fisher who has a dog that only eats kippers

Tom McConnachie

Big brown eyes that twinkle and shine,
once stared pitifully into mine.
How could anyone be so unkind
to a little dog who's so sublime?

You didn't want me at the start,
but now you trust me with all your heart.
Running around the garden where you belong
is what you love doing all day long.

Lying in my arms like a teddy bear,
you fall asleep without a care.
Oh little black poodle so small and cute
your yap is like a howling flute!

So thanks to the couple who didn't care,
and didn't have the love to spare
for a little dog, who to me,
is my special 'Little B'.

Eda Hughes

Mole

I'm a whiskery mole
and I live in a hole
and I'm known as Raoul
at the 'Tunnel and Roll'
cos I burrow about
keep extending my home
so that nobody knows
if I'm home or I roam

When they tread on my ceiling
or rake up the ground
I can hear all their scratchings
but make not a sound.
Then at night I crawl out
of my spirally mound
and I nibble their seedlings
and scuttle around

I do digs in the moonlight
with other furred friends
and we dance to the fireflies
from dusk to night's end
but by dawn I creep back
to my deep-seated hole
where I curl up and sleep
in my warm earthy home

Rosemary Keith

Coco

You are what you are Coco, a lump of chocolate
Velvety and smooth on the outside and sweet on the inside
Your first two years of life weren't good
Now you have us and we have you
You may not be able to see us but I know you can smell us and hear us
Your favourite time is mealtime, once it's in the bowl, two minutes later it's gone
You love going for a walk, you're now in a routine
Once you're outside your nose goes down and away you go
Lots of new smells out there for you to enjoy, something you didn't have before
Guided by us not to bump into trees and lamp posts, across the roads we go
Certain noises make you jump, a bus going by makes you cower
Time to turn round and make our way home
You have sniffed your path this way before and soon we are through the door
Straight to the water bowl for a long deserved drink
Time for sleep on the nearest cushion
Soon you're asleep as we hear your happy snore
We love you Coco for evermore.

Suzanne King

Cat's Whispers

Standing coyly in the lamplight, with a sensual and charismatic glance
wide opened eyes begin a conversation
that seems a little more designed by nurture
than by nature, choice or chance.

And observations are not lost within the subtle movements
Just like the Cirrus cloud formations that are blown by the windy weather streams
The communicating glance of the investigative cat is captured
Just like a casual whisper, reflected, by the rainbow in a re-enacted dream.

Where play is seen by humans for deeper reason,
the pleasing senses of the feline are heightened just for fun.
And just as the social glue will hold the ragged edge of life together
The cat will purr with pure excitement until the horizon and the darkness are as one.

That run like colours on the palette of the artist
as he paints from the dancing eye line to her stare
as she closes in to build on instinct and emottion,
we capture the fascination of a feline love affair.

That lies beyond the bond that can't be broken,
Is a token of affection and spoken words that rhyme
The cat's acrobatic skills have poise and prowess
like a circus act whose lives add up to nine

Alan Glendinning

Spider

We'll hang amongst the nothingness
that's holding up the sky,
and play the part of planets
where the comets come to die.
And asteroids in death throes,
as they stumble through their dust,
enfold us in their splendour
and then are truly trussed.

Alice Keel

The Dog On The Hill

Laying,
In the grass
On the hill
Time,
It will surpass.

Bang.
What was that?
A noise.
A shot.
He's scared
And off he trots.

Up the hill
Through the grass
Back to where I'm waiting.

He shoots to the side,
Under the grass,
Where he hides.
By the rock,
And the tree
And that was when,
He spotted me.

And so he stayed,
For a while,
Until I took him home,
That's when he smiled.

Rowan Boardley (14)

My 'Little' Puppy

My dog's name is Charlie
His middle name is Zeus,
And if we can help it
We never let him loose.

He runs under the tables
And round and round the chairs,
Leaving my disgruntled mum
To hoover up his hairs.

He's really very playful
And really loves his food,
Yet when he sees our big fat cat
They both get in a mood.

Charlie is a mixed breed
Of four types of dogs we think,
So he's nowhere near a pedigree
And can reach up to our sink.

The dogs that we assume
Have made this playful pup,
Are German Shepherd, Rottie, Doberman
And a Lab who is growing up.

He is a very handsome dog
But now just wait and see,
The best thing of all about this lad
Is he belongs to *me!*

Kathleen Garrett (12)

In Memory Of Garfield

Mostly no one noticed you were even there,
Yet you are present in every memory for which I care
The years of brave fighting are now over and done
Loved and remembered you rest knowing that you won

Mostly no one noticed you were even here
But you were present in every moment I hold dear
We fought the last fight with little more to gain
But now your spirit is free from suffering and pain

Sandi has been waiting for you on the Rainbow Bridge
For such a long time . . .
And she will take care of you now

We all feel like there is a massive hole in the family . . .
Love from big brother Matthew, little sister Misty and Mummy xxx

Jayne Walker

Unconditional Love

I own a dog called Bramble
Who means the world to me,
A black and white collie who's just turned three.
His eyes are like mirrors and tell me his moods,
They go large and bright when naughty
And soft when he is good.
He loves his walks and playing ball,
With pals around the park,
He'd stay there for hours on end
Even in the dark.
He's a true and faithful friend as everyone can see,
Unconditional love he gives, especially to me.

Morag McIntosh

To Rufus

To Rufus
Advice not followed.

'Irish setters? Beautiful dogs.
Never, ever, have one.'

A thirteen year long experience.

At last comes July.
He sits, king of the castle.
Wistfully, pups look.

Homeward. In the car
Handkerchiefs clutched to noses.
Windows open wide.

Mother's milk helps bring bonding and great joy.
Oh, how we bonded, my beautiful boy.
For one happy week you bounded around
Then found some noxious substance on the ground.
The vet looked worried and shook his grave head.
'He is very ill. Try to keep him fed.'
Wriggling body protesting on my lap,
I tried to put calf's foot jelly on tap.
Arms, hands, face, hair, thickly covered in stick,
Whilst praying, thinking, '*He must not be sick.*'
Four days later, you determined to mend,
Before I, finally, went round the bend.

Extract from a training manual.
'Irish setters are very difficult to train.
They are highly intelligent with a will of their own'.

Off we set, you and I, in harmony
And peace, to attend our doggy classes.
Pregnant, I went hopefully and calmly,
You, all set for the first of your farces.
'Hold the rope and call him. Pull him to you.'
I obeyed. You, hurtled across the room,
Passed me, ignored me. The rope burns were few.
I was left standing, all ready to fume.
'Say stay. With authority call his name.'
I called. You skidded, halted, looked at me.
Tug of war, glorious, marvellous game.
Now, on hands and knees, I wanted to flee.
We leave, as the thought through my mind passes,
'Woman gives birth at dog training classes'.

The best of pals, Harry Cornish appears,
Two hearing aids firmly clamped in his ears.
'Let Rufus go. Let us help make his day.'
With great reluctance, we slowly obey.
An arrow of fire, Rufus finds his mark,
Hearing aids fly, not to be found till dark.
Great paws straddling Harry's shoulders in love,
Gentle red bomber, as sweet as a dove.

Sadly, we watched, as time moved too quickly.
His coat, which outshone pre-Raphaelite copper,
Vibrant, vivid, richly glowing,
Became, like the embers of ancient fires,
Dry, dull and greyly brittle.
His unique, engaging Mickey Mouse smile,
Still endearing,
But now, finally, enclosed in a silver muzzle.
We visualised him racing, all hurdles leaping,
With tongue hanging out,
Tail, ears streaming.
An elongated streak of pure animal joy.
Not sitting, waiting, to be lifted o'er stiles.
The cries of, 'I'll kill him,' no longer rang out
As, much like a frightened, bewildered child,
He sat ever closer for comfort and dreaming.
More and more he held up his paw
For us to hold in a loving clasp.
His glorious, tempestuous joie de vivre parted,
And, we knew, that his passing had slowly started.
Our faithful, wild and wonderful boy.

We had not followed the best advice.

Pamela Hall

Millie

Sit Millie, stay Millie, jump in the air,
Mainly her attitude is 'I don't care!'

She may be tiring,
She may not listen,
But at least she has never ever gone missin'.

She's so fluffy,
She's so big,
All she does is dig, dig, dig!

She'll chew your socks
And chew your shoes,
So you get all of the clues.

Yes, she is hungry,
We give her food,
Finally she is in a great mood.

She may not be perfect,
With her crazy mind,
But she is certainly one of a kind.

Charlotte Barker (16)

Norman My Pet Fly

I sit so still and wonder why
He went away with no goodbye.
I miss the buzz of tiny wings,
The rectangular dance under light fittings.

Perhaps he's found his sugar cube
Or's stuck inside an M&M's tube
In someone's pocket on a train
On the way to the airport to catch a plane.

Maybe he's glued to a toffee apple
In the audience of a wrestling grapple,
Or maybe's visited Liz the spider
And now's wriggling and squiggling and tickling inside her.
Or perhaps just drowned in half a cider,
Or's giving lessons to hang-gliders.

No more shall I witness the simple fun
Of a proboscis inserted in a sticky bun
Now summer days just pass me by
Without my pet Norman the fly.

Richard Leach

Smoky

I'd looked under the table, then under my chair,
Could not find my funny old cat anywhere!
'Come on Smoky,' I called. 'It's time to put you out,'
Carried on looking and then I began to shout.

Perhaps into another room he may have run?
My lovely: long grey, big ball, bundle of fur fun.
In all four bedrooms I gave a quick all round glance,
I wonder if he's got stuck in wardrobes by chance.

But then I heard a prolonged noise by the back door,
Which was where, I found my feline, giving loud roar.
The door hastily opened, with one purr Smoky fled,
To make fresh holes in my newly dug flower bed.

Susan Mullinger

Who Is This?

She sits on my lap
disturbs my nap
she's black and hairy
in the dark she's scary
cuddly and small
however not very tall
scared of dogs
loves fish
in a very big dish
last time she chased a mouse
unfortunately ruined my house
she can jump very high
always ruins my tie
scratches the walls
miaow she calls

She is a cat.

Arooj Javaid Khan Lodhi

O What A Cute Pussycat

My playful feral cat,
All tied up in cotton lace,
With wool, string and cardboard
Ferreting around in plastic bags,

O what a cute pussycat Harry is,
While chasing daisies and flies,
With insects and mice,
Suddenly Harry comes alive,

While climbing the sycamore tree,
After birds, bees and wasps,
Into the neighbour's garden he goes,
Creeping with his outstretched toes,

Claws at the ready,
While stalking a large black crow,
You would think that Harry was harmless,
But he was clever like a vulpine fox,

As he played in the cardboard box,
Biding his time for a clever catch,
As all the birds warned each other,
The owl that Harry couldn't match,

O what a cute pussycat Harry is,
As the hedgehog crossed the lawn,
Eating all his cat food,
In the early hours of dawn,

As Harry miaowed at the moon,
He would hide and dart,
In the dining room,
Eating sachet after sachet of food,

And while the household slept,
He would be stalking the garden gnome,
Likened to the biggest jungle cat,
While the poet who wrote this, fled to Rome.

James S Cameron

What A Thrill

What a thrill seeing a squirrel demonstrate its
Instinctive skill, balletically dancing on
Pine palings, its dance floor railings.
Nowhere to be seen any failings.
Watching its antics we adore, and cry encore
Wishing for more, completely enjoying its terpsichore
Its bushy tail waving yet balancing
The little body in the breeze.
This scene set on a golf course,
Wild the squirrel, small part of
Nature's wonderful tour de force.
Men can but envy such physical
Supremacy. Approach to this creature
And to a treetop it will swiftly steer,
Scampering vertically, spirally, does disappear.
Do not forget they perform without a safety net.
Their skill so assured to danger they are inured.
As into trouble they are never lured.
'Nimblenuts' my name for grey bushy-tailed
Creature, which in the wild is such an engaging
Feature. Ever active and extremely attractive
Yet I have regrets for since from
America being introduced, the population of
The little red squirrel has been severely reduced.
Moreover its habitat is to but a few places confined,
While older generations can recall observing it
Countrywide, so it almost smacks of genocide.
How to redress the balance is difficult to decide,
One is drawn to the gentle red variety, for its
Dainty charm, and that allied to the fact that it is
Native to our isle, and has such neat and elegant style.
To cull the grey population and limit its
Territorial domination appears to be a potential
Proposition, yet one which would surely generate
Fierce opposition. Hence we are left with a
Conundrum, and search for
A solution that is not hum-drum.
Alas! When with nature interferes
Into muddy waters he steers.

Animal Antics 2011

Now many wish that grey squirrels
Were left in the USA, sadly that
Is hindsight and too late in the day.
Maybe the active greys should be returned to the
United States to resume their original ways.

Graham Watkins

World Of Animals

Today we drove just twenty-two miles to a conservation zoo,
We walked along Savannah Tracks, a boardwalk giving a nice view,
The Buffalo and Antelope look good, and dainty is the Deer,
All the animals are threatened species, that is why they are here,
The Cheetah was roaming around, the Amur Tigers were dozing,
The Leopard was on the prowl, and the Humboldt Penguin was posing,
We gazed at the Giraffes in their large enclosure busy browsing,
The Macaque was swinging well, and the Snow Leopard needed rousing,
Przewalki's Horses came over to have their photograph taken,
For all the animals this conservation zoo is a haven,
Gibbons were moving swiftly while Pygmy Hippos were moving slow,
My favourite bird in this zoo is the beautiful Pink Flamingo,
The Lemurs' home is quite big, their two cascades make a lovely sight,
Birds we saw, Secretary, Black Swan, Mandarin, but none in flight,
The Owls were half asleep, but Wallabies ran free, how they could go,
A beautiful scene is the lake with fountain and weeping willow,
It was good to see there's even a home for the elusive Bat,
Because they're cute my favourite animal of all is the Meerkat,
A Hornbill was building a nest, while Kangaroos lay in the shade,
On the back of a Cotton-top Tamarin a young baby laid,
The Camels got up for a walk, and elsewhere Zebras were grazing,
The Maras, Capybaras and Tapirs and Rhinos were lazing,
Servals were having some shut-eye, the Coati was on the roof,
I wanted to take the Chipmunk home, these small animals I love,
Passing regularly was the attractive road train and rail train,
It's handy for people, I looked out for them coming round again,
Adding to the zoo life scenery were flowering cherry trees,
On this hot April day we just strolled like everyone else at ease,
Our trip to see the animals on this nice day had been pleasant,
Marwell Zoological Park is interesting. I'm glad we went.

Gill Coombes

Amber eyes and runny nose,
Always keeps us on our toes.

Curly tail and camel's feet,
Always begging for a treat.

Runner's legs and ears so wide,
Finds us when we try to hide.

Greets hello with a jump and a lick,
Calming her down, that's the trick.

Loves to cuddle her toy lamb,
In her basket, she tries to cram.

Cheers us up when we're feeling down,
Always acting like a clown.

There's nothing about her we would change,
No substitute, no pet exchange,
Her smelly breath, her moulting hair,
That silly dog, our Darcy Bear.

Wynona Lodge

A Poem For Toffee

Toffee is a name which will always remind me of happiness and joy,
the love, trust and honour you have shown to me forever will let your courage
and bravery shine like a star, forever your love will stay in my heart and all
of your happiest moments will stay with me for the rest of my life.

The caring, happiness and joy, your love, trust and honour, the bravery
and courage you have shown to me prove you have and always
will be there for me, a true friend and my very best friend.

The stars in the sky shine brightly, but have never shone as bright as your golden coat of fur,
Dewdrops in the morning sparkle in the sunlight, but are
never as shiny as your diamond-like eyes,
Treacle and golden syrup is sweet, but is never as sweet as you are.

If I ever get upset, sad or hurt, I will think of your happiness,
I will dream about us playing in the garden together, and
will play the piano with love and kindness,
You are my best friend, the best animal in the world and my wonderful dog Toffee.

Grace Palmer

Animal Acrostic - Penguin

P enguins are birds but they do not fly
E ggs that lay on the ground undercover and dry
N eatly dressed, they look clean and bright
G racefully groomed, recognised by voice and sight
U nderwater they swim to catch their food
I cy lands they prefer, in a pleasant mood
N early wearing a tuxedo, they look so good

Foqia Hayee

A Tribute To Nissi

Although the sands of time keep turning,
My mind often wanders back to your loving face,
Your little quirks and mad spurts of energy,
The time when your beauty graced the Earth.

The first day I held you in my arms,
My mother told me I was getting a white jumper,
How true was that statement?
You were a white ball of fur.

From a puppy until you were fully grown,
You fell in love with us as us with you,
Part of the family but so much more,
You were more than a best friend to us.

You used to jump up on the sofa,
And run around and around the coffee table,
Making the buzzing sound,
You were completely barking mad.

You wore out many a soft toy,
With your wild and crazy antics,
You must have thought you were human,
What a sight when you had spaghetti chops!

Lots of memories,
We are forever indebted to you,
For choosing us as your family,
And for keeping the smiles on our faces constant!

Kimberly Davidson

Paws For Thought

Come Lily this should do the trick,
Let's get our human just to sit,
For she keeps walking round and round,
Her feet - they seldom touch the ground!
In circles she chases her own tail,
Enough to make us kittens wail -
Unlike us when in a spin,
Come Lily, this way we all win!

You on her knee, me in the chair,
So she can cuddle and we can purr.

'It seems my girls have again got their own way,
Until they decide to eat or play.
I really don't know what to think,
As they look at me and then they wink!'

There Gracie, we have done the trick,
We've got our human just to sit -
And write for us a little poem,
So she won't feel so forlorn.
For she feels lost without her gift with words -

When words get lost, where do they go?
Or where do words come from - does anyone know?

Purrhaps it is the purr of our love,
Or the purr of our prayers?
Do us cats know or does anyone care!

Is there a difference do you think?
(And they give each other a knowing wink!)
Come on Lily - you know
We ow we ow we ow . . .

Roughly translated
Purr could read as power of . . .

Loosely translated we ow we ow we ow
Is an interpretation of
Me ow me ow me ow
Just so, dear reader, if you are not a cat lunatic (like our human mum)
You understand!

Gracie & Lily Richards

Harry

(Dedicated to Nikola Lawson and her beloved Labrador Harry)

I'm really
Going to miss you
My boy, my loyal friend
I'm going
To miss the company
We shared from birth to end

The walks
We shared together
Both in the sun and rain
Now each
Passing season
Will never seem the same

I'm going
To miss the cuddles
The greetings at the door
The sound
Of your voice barking
And your presence that's for sure

I'm going
To miss you Harry
My golden Labrador
My friend
And great companion
Rest in peace and bon voyeur

Barbara C Perkins

Home From Home (Davo)

It's early morning
I shiver as the stiff breeze
Blows through my fur
And the cold ground
Cools my feet
Click goes the lock
A hand rubs behind my ear
'See you tonight Davo'
I sit there blinking
As the car drives off to work
This could be a problem
However this smart cat
Has got it licked
Over the fence
A quick stroll
To next-door's back door
A plaintive - miaow
Or two
The door opens
Warm air rushes out
And envelops me
Two arms scoop me up
And cradle me
A rub behind my ears
Accompanied by a gentle cluck
Of course I show my appreciation
And purr until we both quiver
Then my adoptive mum
Gently puts me down
With a nonchalant air
I stroll
Towards the welcoming couch
One last glance
Then off to sleep
To dream
Of bowls filled with tasty treats
Until once more
It's time to go home

June F Taylor

Milly

She is quick
To defend
Her master in thin or thick
Her love does mend.

She licks my hand
Her insistence to get out
And into the park:
It's her land
In her demonstration - 'no doubt'
As humans hide in the 'dark'!

She's quiet
Her master and mistress
Rest, after a long week
And she?
Meek as ever
I'm not too clever
But I'm sure
God will cherish her forever.

Such a kind and determined doggy
So loveable
And happy
And gentle
Yet no one, small as she is, can enter
Their domain
Unless they will it so
And then she loves
As surely as
Time must go!

Ricl Jia

The Little Sloth

Two sloths halfway up a tree
in a forest far away.
A little one, very sleepy,
half-heard an adult say:
'We had a giant ancestor . . .
Little one, this is no time to snore!'

The two of them hung upside down.
Their toehold was secure.
The adult wore a worried frown:
'I do hope there's a cure
that prevents a further shrinkage . . .
. . . we're at a critical stage . . .

Once we sloths were as tall as trees
whose top leaves we could reach.
Little one, did I hear you sneeze?
Attention while I teach
you how by this generation
we are such a shrunken nation.

Now we have to climb up a tree,
gaze at the forest floor
which does curtail our liberty.
We're smaller than before -
But what I cannot help thinking
is that we sloths still are shrinking!'

Fast to his branch near the tree trunk
the little sloth could hear
how his once great nation had shrunk
and might soon disappear -
But how big he was - or how small
he really did not care at all.

For him to be slothful enough.
A state to last - and last.
Not so much shrinking as thinking
but slowly - not too fast.
Surely for sloths always some room?
Adults too full of gloom and doom.

Christine Mary Creedon

A Day In The Zoo

'Don't forget,' said the elephant, 'we open at ten'
'I'll be ready,' said the hippo, 'to look at all the men'
'Now behave,' said the zebra, 'men have feelings too
You know it can't be easy, living in a zoo'

'I feel so sorry for the people,'
Said a smiling crocodile
'They have square and ugly faces
And an awful sense of style

I very nearly ate one, on the visit yesterday
Sitting minding my own business I overheard one say
That I was very pretty, but they would much prefer
To make of me a handbag and turn brown bear into fur'

'Well the cheeky little rascal' said the lion to the ape
'I would do the same to them but their skin's a funny shape'
'Don't worry,' said Jemima, a beautiful giraffe
'Let's put our heads together, play a prank to make us laugh'

'I cannot leave the water,' honked a little sea lion pup
'Let me do some splashing to wind the people up
Croc you kiss the parrot, while the meerkat has a ride
Do some forward rolls and ballet, on the rhino's big backside'

'I will kiss the lion,' said Priscilla the giraffe
'Now hyenas when this happens do try not to laugh
We will mystify the humans, confuse their tiny brains
Send them all home thinking
That the world as gone insane.'

Lynn Elizabeth Noone

My Butterfly

The butterfly landed on my hand gently
It had beautiful wings that were as red as a ruby
And it had many decorations on its beautiful wings
It flapped its wings slowly
And its antennae looked really amazing and extremely vast
The beautiful, big butterfly beamed away
And then came back into my hand
It had a yellow outline and four big green emerald spots.

Gbolahan Awonaiya (9)

Toby One

He's a wee dog, by that I mean small
Kind of squat and chunky, certainly not tall.
But when it comes to the doggy personality stakes
Our Toby is big, he really has what it takes.

His eyes are deep brown, big brown pools
He questions you with them, he thinks humans are fools.
He kinda cocks his head on one side and looks straight
I have to laugh cos he's my best mate.

Riding in the car is one of his favourite times
You just say 'ride' and in he climbs.
Then it's head out the window for that blast of fresh air
With a smile on his face, he has nerry a care.

The only thing that surpasses the vehicle ride
Is when you pick up his lead and head outside.
There's no need to say anything, no need to talk
He's not silly, he knows it's time for a walk.

When no one's home he's always on guard
Whether it's inside the house or up the backyard.
He's loving, intelligent, a whole lot of fun
We all love him to bits and call him - Toby One.

Jonathan Tromane

Ebby And I

Ebby and I have grown together
As time has passed us by
My beautiful intelligent Lab
Which no one can deny
She takes care of my grandchildren
While swimming in the sea
She swims beside to keep them safe
And brings them safely back to me
She is good and kind to everyone
A delight to have around
She loves to be by my side
No better friend could I have found
The thing she most enjoys in life
Is to swim and jump the waves
She romps and plays upon the beach
Like a pup is how she behaves
I know that when she's gone
I'll stare out across the sea
I'll see my Ebby swimming
For she'll always be with me

Catherine M Armstrong

That One Eye

I have a love with just one eye,
She lost the other when a car passed by.

When I get home from work at night,
Though I may have called in for a pint.

My love is waiting there for me,
She needs a feed, she needs a pee.

Then she sits down by the door,
And I know there's one job more.

So off we go come rain or shine,
Then I know she will be fine.

She'll smell the grass, yes every blade,
While I stand there in the rain.

Then she'll turn around to go,
Homeward bound with me in tow.

When we're back she'll have a shake,
Before a towel I can take.

Then she'll lie down as if to die,
But it's always open that one eye.

William Shire

Lilly

Loveable that's me
Intelligent too.
Like a gazelle when I play . . .
Chase at a fast pace.
Lilly is my name
You'll be dazzled by my sweet personality.
Shy at times I can be . . .
But I love to be brushed
And to snuggle up by a hot bottle
Under Mummy's blankets.

Jessica Stephanie Powell

Poem For My Boys

(In loving memory of Gnasher & Josh)

Two little funny ferret boys,
How you filled my days in endless ways.
I often think of the games we played.

Riding the waves, a blanket on my legs,
Holding your tail gently so you don't fall,
You shake, rattle and laugh.
Then it's time for your bath.

Jumping in the air with glee
Oh good, a treat, sultanas for my tea!
Juggling a ball with your back legs
And spinning round and round . . .
Me laughing at your antics, joy abounds!

You playfully ride your towel gliding up and down the kitchen floor.
Two distinct individual voices chuckling together,
Partners in crime
Who says animals can't laugh?

The snow has fallen deep and crisp
You leap and twist
Catching snowballs -
Otter-like you surf
My heart is filled with love.
Thank you for making me laugh!

And now my heart must break in two,
One half for each of you.
I can't believe by some cruel twist,
I'm losing you both to a genetic fate.
I must be strong and care for you,
Not for myself.

I kiss you both goodbye,
2 weeks and 2 days inbetween
You loved each other so . . .
And you love me, I know.

It's time to let you go
And set your spirits free
To a place where you will no longer suffer.
You will stay in my heart and mind for the rest of my time.

N Brocks

Whiskey's Poem

Whiskey was a beauty and loved
So very, very much,
He had the loudest purr I ever heard
Sounded by just a single touch.
His handsome face would light up rooms
And we'd all stop and stare,
With his Cheshire grin he had always been
The one to whom cats would compare.
'Your cat is such a solid tom
But he's not a hunter.'
That we already knew cos it was true
And a lazy cat no wonder.
He'd sleep all day on any bed
And roam around at night.
But never went far and walked on our cars
And now I say goodbye.

Laura Martin

A Dog's Life

Sanka Sam is my name,
Now happy and free, I can play the game,
Though my legs should be four, I have only three
Because humans were horrid and cruel to me.
For seven sad years I lived this way,
Unhappy, starving and beaten each day;
I longed to be loved and given a home
But to find it many a mile I had to roam.
Then at last I was there,
Oh lucky me!
I'm loved, so loved by Gilly you see.

Gillian Ann Potter

Don't Leave Me

So this is the reason I am here -
this is what they do.
He was kind to me.
He examined my back legs
I cried and tried to tell him.
She was holding me
and stroking my face,
tears dripping down onto my fur
like rain from leaves on the trees
in my beloved garden.
She signed a piece of white rustly paper,
then he gave me an injection.
I began to feel warm and fuzzy.
The pain in my legs began to recede.
She kept stroking me
and talking to me
but the only words I heard were,
'Don't leave me - I love you.
I've loved you every day for thirteen and a half years
and I don't want to be without you.'
So this is what they do.

She bent over me and whispered.
I didn't feel the second injection much,
but my beloved garden appeared,
sunlight rustling the leaves.
She was standing by my wooden bench
cuddling me in her arms
and I knew she'd never leave me . . .

Vivien Steels

Cat Nose And Holiday

(House- and cat-sitting in the family home)

You don't fool me,
cat nose stuffed under the gate,
pseudo-tiger pacing the kitchen floor!
I remember you, little kitten,
laughable ball of fur
falling from the tops of armchairs,
upturned white belly,
legs fingering the sky.
And now do you complain
that we have robbed you of your catness?

Silly ginger tom!
Just think of all the catfood in the larder,
the price of being uncat!
And do we all protest
about the mutilated
trounced-mouse torsos
on the lawn?
Flimsy furry toys that come apart
like balls of wool?

Oh cat! Uncat fat anticat!
Befuddled thin fatcat!
The house is under new management.

Do mandarins keep ponderous
nonsense cats in China?
(I ask questions like this
because it mystifies me so
to see you at the front door
waiting for them all
to come home.)

Jeff Vinter

The Barking Cat

While standing on the doorstep
And drinking tea that night,
I saw a group of nasty cats
All looking for a fight

They circled round the garden
And gently closing in,
They sniffed around the plant pots
And round our wheelie bin

And then they found their victim
Young Wesley standing by,
She curled into a little ball
And covered up her eyes

Surrounding Wesley, mean and claws
Upon her they did gang,
My eyes and ears did not believe
For what then did began.

As the gang did then approach her
All surly, mean and tough,
Young Wesley arched her head back
And loudly cried out, 'Woof!'

As the cats did quickly scarper
And out of sight to see,
I stood there in a state of shock
While choking on my tea

So now we feed her other things
Not Whiskas, fish or mouse,
We give her only dog food
And let her guard the house.

Rick Bywater

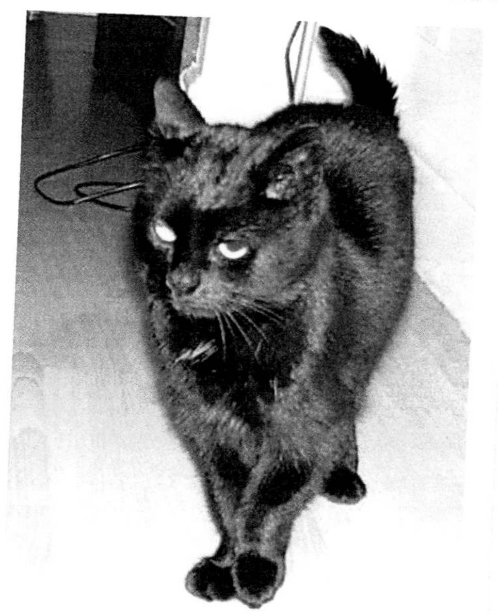

A Tale Of Two Cats

As different as chalk and cheese
in all your ways, in cat-like looks,
Nelson with your nose held high,
with ginger coat of silken fur,
Oscar with your humble ways,
black and white and cotton strong.

One of timid nature, and one of
self-sure will,
Each little way, I see each day,
is growing more and more,
into a contest for to win,
the upper hand and rule.

So Nelson keep your fur on,
and Oscar keep your cool,
As you both know when doggies
chase, a team you'll need to be,
As enemies you may lose,
together you can win.

And now I say of you dear Nelson,
Your great dislike of dirty paws,
of other cats and garden soil,
and wrong brand foods and
Oscar's presence, your pedigree
does you no great credit.

I put aside your haughty ways
thief of my emotions, and
remember when I met you,
in your rescued chamber,
Among the rest I liked you best,
for your spirit and your pride.

And so my friend, my wayward
puss, I waiver any thought,
to put to flight, your sheer delight,
Of naughty wilful spite and claw,
and settle for your nature.

Dearest little Oscar, you take
it in your stride, when faced
with each rejection, it does not
matter why, your hero he will
always be, you copy all his moves,

and follow just behind.

You took a while to come inside,
you waited for the turn of tide,
It took a bite to make you choose,
the devil or the deep, and in you
came to face the foe, in friendly
cat-like gesture.

A heart went out to greet you,
my own, but not the furry kind,
Poor gentle soul, and so afraid,
of shadow and of hand, you
lingered by your fellow shape,
who spat and hissed and clawed.

But you just shook and followed,
and gave way to his whims,
At meals you would not eat elsewhere,
so had to share the fare.
Tolerance set in two years hence,
and now you're settled well.

You come back from the hunt, and
share the captured prey, he is your
buddy then, and proud you are to help
him in his older years regain his
youthful play, he does not blink an
eyelid then, for that moment - friends.

You love the hugs and kisses, the
stroking and attention,
He wants no fuss and just prefers,
to put his paws upon my lap,
and sit upon my form in bed,
Your ventures have yet to run to this.

Teresa Kerry

Poppy The Thorn

Stalking the streets or snoozing on the floor, my cat is one that you have to adore.
As sweet as a baby or as fierce as a lion, my heart will always melt in her presence.
During the day she is curled up on my lap, but during the
night she moves with the stealth of a bat.
Her fur as dark as raven, her eyes as emerald as gems.
Sitting tall and proud on her perch like an Egyptian sphinx
waiting for intruders that may lurch into her domain.

A fellow feline comes paddling on the scene, watch as she
goes bounding towards it looking tough and mean!
Lurking by the door as the post arrives, tall, bushy, eyes fixated on the prize.
Nothing can sway her and for that reason I will never betray her.
As agile as a swan or as inept as a mole, her personality has a lot of diversity as a whole.
At night her dark fur masks her from piercing eyes, a master of disguise.

When she hears the sound of rattling like a black cloud, she will come storming into view.
Like a tiger she will come running for her prey, growling defensively as she ravages
her food to nothing, warding off her enemies, ordering them not to disobey.
She is heavy to the touch, but she looks as statuesque as a ballerina.
As solid as an oak and as wise as an owl.
Strong, robust and stern.

Down by the pond lounging lazily in the sun, bathing in the warmth like a queen.
Eyes virulent to spot her quarry, her head snapping forward.
Immediately she is on her feet, paw poised, claws extended.
Her head whirls round at the sound of shouting, as Mother
raises to save the water-bound victim.
Her eyes scold into hers, outraged at being cheated the kill.

All cats come with quirks to fit their owner's own,
Poppy and I are like two pieces of a jigsaw.
She came with a classical choice, whiskers, ears, tail
and four paws with five razor-like claws.
She is truly a killer cat and that is that.

Emily Davison

Daydreaming

(For Ruskin)

If I could fly,
I'd make my dreams come true.
I'd fly to the top of a house,
sprawl on the ridge tiles
and bask in the sun.

If I could fly,
I'd nest in a tree,
pretending to sleep -
but secretly keeping
a ready eye open.

If I could fly,
I'd wreak havoc in the air
among those nasty birds,
showing them just what
one cat can *really* do.

Gordon Jackson

My Dog Coco

I have a dog named Coco,
And sure at times she seems a little loco.
But she is one of a kind,
And every now and then she proves she was quite the find.
Spends all day running free,
Full of happiness and glee.
If only she could learn to calm down,
And quit acting like a clown.
Though it does fill me with cheer,
To see her so happy with no signs of a tear.

Six months, she was when we got her,
A Labrador with chocolate-coloured fur.
Wild and crazy,
You definitely couldn't call her lazy.
She runs and runs for evermore,
She must have one almighty core.
Her big puppy-dog eyes light up whenever it is time to play,
And trust me she could all day, every day.
Now and then, she likes to rest,
So tomorrow she can be at her best.

She is cuddly and cute,
Although at times, she acts like a right brute.
Centre of attention is where she likes to be,
But when she sits on top of you it's quite hard to see.
Dangerous and tough, she may appear,
Really all she is, is gentle and sweet, just with no fear.
She may frighten some,
But all she wants is to be loved and have fun.
My dog Coco is my friend,
For always even at the end.

Sara Burr

My Cat

A plaintive miaow comes from beyond
The bedroom door
My train of thought is disturbed
The grey light of dawn
Percolates through the curtains
I rise and go to the door
She is sitting on the landing
Her green eyes stare up at me questioningly
Slowly she rises on her haunches
Peers hesitantly around the door
Expecting to find an unknown adversary
Confidence returns
She enters the room
Her face, neck and shoulders
Stroke along the edge of the chest of drawers
She then indulges in her favourite mischief
Laying at full stretch
She digs her sharp needle-like claws
Into the fabric beneath the bedboxes
And pulls herself along
I give her a sharp scolding
Like a jack-in-the-box
She springs up and retreats
The pad of paws on the stairs
With a yawn I follow
Dressing gown hanging open
She is in the kitchen

Sitting expectantly by her empty bowl
Breakfast time
The message shining in her eyes.

Terence Leslie Iceton

The Father

The lady took her pure bred bitch
To meet a pure bred male
To get some pure bred puppies
But here's the sorry tale
Her dog it went and slipped her lead
My dog ran after her
I know my dog of old, and
His intentions they were clear
He came back sometime later
His chest puffed up with pride
The lady's dog came trotting back
And she seemed satisfied
The woman's going to sue me
Her language most unkind
I said, 'You know dogs will be dogs
And they say love is blind
You cannot blame me really
It's no good being bitter
I'm sure you'll grow to love
Those mongrels in the litter.'

G Andrews

Sloppy Tongue

Sloppy tongue
leaving a trail of dew.
Wakes me from my slumber
like a cold pool on a hot summer's day.
Sloppy tongue
is the perfect mop
for a sudden sticky spill.
Just don't tell Mom!
Sloppy tongue
sometimes gets into the strangest places.
Makes the strangest faces,
and loves to eat the strangest tastes.
And when no one else can sense it,
sloppy tongue gives the loveliest wet kisses.

Patricia Ferraiuolo

St Michael's Mount

The great day dawned by popular demand,
The first day of the first race meet to run in this fair land
and many more to come no doubt
to the joy of many a stable tout.
With pious thoughts and pounding heart
St Michael led his charger 'Grace'
champing at the bit towards the start.
God would see him past the post -
the righteous in first place.
(Unknown to him though, God had other plans
and he would have a nasty fall from grace.)
So with a mighty roar the shout went up and off they went at speed.
St Michael clinging gamely, to his snorting, galloping steed.
White robe flowing out behind, beard flapping in his face.
Eyes ablaze with manic missionary zeal
he slashed the flanks with sharpened spur protruding from his heel.
Now Grace, she was a jumper, and she jumped with power and pace
but she was getting left behind in this particular race.
Each soaring leap she lost another yard.
God, thought Michael, *this is bloomin' hard*
and so too was the ground on which he landed when he fell
head first with agonising shouts of pain
only to be dragged along all tangled in the rein.
And as he struggled loose, all bruised and with a fractured knee
Grace, she went on jumping, riderless and free
in her own time, in her own space,
the only jumper in the first flat race.

Ben Corde

Here To Stay

He arrived in my garden
One morning in May.
'Oh look there's a cat,'
I heard someone say.
I wonder if he's got a home,
Or a cat that just likes to roam.
They all gather round
With much ooing and ahing
Don't let it in.
The door they are barring.
Perhaps it's got fleas
Or something that's catching.
You can tell by his looks
He's already been scratching.
Both his ears are in a tatty condition.
No, you can't go inside you've not had permission.
Let's give him a drink and food,
And see if he's in a friendly mood.
Now that I'm feeling full and well-fed
A sleep would be nice in a soft cosy bed.
The door's been left open,
I've had a good meal,
If I behave well I've got a good deal.
I'll just put on a friendly show,
No telling how far all this fuss will go.
What a comfy armchair
Dare I try it out?
Hope that they won't give my ear a good clout.
Oh look how he's all curled up in the chair
It looks like he's always been there.
Now that I'm in they won't turn me away,
I knew right from then, I was *here to stay.*

Margaret Sparrow

Humans mark territory with fences and communicate mainly with words.
Grey tiger-striped Patches, cat-watchman with notched ears, sprays trees, flowers
and house walls, his perpendicular tail an exclamation mark against intruders.
But indoors he spares our French sofa with horsehair, and my
German feather bedding, even antique table and chair legs.
Panther-black Aladdin, fierce warrior, lays his trophy, a baby pigeon, at my doorstep,
then retracts his sharp weapons into soft padded washcloths,
and sprawls in a spot of sunlight on the oriental rug
where he spit-slicks his coat until it shines like aged mahogany.
Sleek orange-coated Easter, goddess of our feline household, keeps time for us all.
Come 6pm, the News Hour, she waits at the entrance to the TV room where
my lap welcomes her warm body, more soothing than a hot water bottle.
Scrawny white-haired Tiny, queen of hearts, snuggling against my mother's chest,
purring in unison with her laboured breathing,
was present at her last breath while I had fallen asleep on my watch.
After my mother's body was removed Tiny jumped back into the sheets,
sniffed for familiar scents and curled up, awaiting my mother's return.
I am late preparing dinner. Delicate Easter rubs her delicate flanks against my calves.
'Hurry up! You'll miss the beginning. The weatherman is already on.'

Ute Carson

The Yorkshire Terrier

Tyke's tiny terrier
What a lovely pet
Toy ones and heavier
Several sizes you can get
By half-stones they may be lighter
Than the average dog of 'Brit'
But stone for stone as fighter
They are not lacking Yorkshire grit.
Even though they are small
Just a tiny scrap
They captivate us all
Except when full of yap.
But that is to tell you
Something you should know
A stranger is approaching
Halfway down the row.
Not for me your wild Rottweilers
Your Mastifs or your hounds
Or dogs from dodgy dealers
That worry posties on their rounds.
I'll keep my little Yorkie
With his captivating charms
That attract lots of company
When I hold him in my arms.
But strangers count your fingers
If you are giving him a stroke
With a hand that too long lingers
With a prodding and a poke
For in spite of chucks and chuckles
He'll reduce you down to knuckles
If he senses you're more a 'moggie'
Than a 'doggie' kind of folk.

V F Clarke-Irons

Pepe The Cat

My name is Pepe
I am black and white
I have my favourite chair
I sometimes go out at night

I do not like rain
Oh what a pain
I do not know what to do
Maybe I will catch a mouse
But I have been told
'Do not bring it in the house'

I enjoy my biscuits
At breakfast I may get toast
I like to lie in the sun
Or run around and have fun
Of course I go to bed

I am well fed
I am a happy cat
With a lovely home
So here I will stay
Enjoy every day
I will never want to roam

Patricia G Stone

Poppet

Our Poppet is a crazy cat
Her favourite toy is an old felt hat
She bats it all around the house
(Most cats prefer a catnip mouse.)

She teases the dogs and makes them flee
By jumping out from behind a tree
She lies on the aviary and frightens the birds
And seems to be mouthing unutterable words
She sits by the pond and tries to catch fish
While totally ignoring the fish in her dish!

One day the cat from No 3 decided to climb our apple tree
He was only a few feet from the ground
When the wicked Poppet came around
Quickly to the tree she ran, and hatched a very cunning plan
If she stayed beneath the tree all day
The little cat couldn't get away.

Afraid to come down he climbed to the top
But twenty-five feet is a long way to drop
And if he lost his footing or put a paw wrong
And landed on Poppy - oops, another life gone!

Tired and frightened he started to mew
Until he was saved by a cat rescue crew
So that was the end of the afternoon's fun
And Poppet strolled off to lie in the sun.

Her beauty is beyond compare with golden eyes and silky hair
White whiskers adorn a jet-black face
She moves with elegance, style and grace
But the pranks she gets up to, we nearly have fits
And although she's so naughty we love her to bits
But the simple truth we have to face, our Poppet is a basket case!

Sheelah Collier-Ringer

One Cat Against The World

Once upon a time,
There was one feline.
A cat against the world.

Known to her humans as Cutie,
(For obvious reasons, but don't be fooled by her cuteness)
But to the Secret Service as Agent QT,
This cat resides in her not-so-secret headquarters . . .
A flower pot in the backyard.

With intense agility and flexibility,
This cat has been trained to perform the most intricate
and lethal moves
To combat the forces of evil.
Using flips through the air
And rolling down the stairs
(And off of my bed ... and off of the little bench in the back garden ...)
Agent QT can defeat any piece of string or insect with wings.

An expert in communications and covert operations,
Agent QT uses her trademark 'Mow' and 'Mah'
(This cat doesn't use the standard 'Miaow')
To get her assets, the humans, to supply her with the most innovative gadgets
Such as Felix cat food sachets and Go-Cat biscuits.

Once kitted-out with Felix,
Agent QT stealthily goes to her window sill watch-point in the living room
Ready to pounce at bathing birds
And other intruders in the front garden
(However unfortunately for her, her efforts are obstructed
by what appears to be a glass force field).

And after a long day of missions,
Cutie returns to her HQ for a final briefing
Before going to her safe-house for a bit of sleeping.
And that is the end of the day for the cat on a mission
The cat against the world.

Sasha Sutton

Richess

As you got ready for eternal sleep,
Your eyes closed for the last time.
The light went out and the spark gone.
But, oh! How the sun shone so bright,
as the angels came down to guide you
along the path to Heaven above.

Where you can shine as bright as
you did on Earth my princess.
May you rest in peace and be at ease,
you are truly loved and greatly missed.
I hope you find another above,
to befriend and love like you were
by all you left behind.

H Wilson

Monkeys They Rule!

M aybe if I could have a pet I wanted.
O h, I think I would choose a monkey!
N either cat nor dog would be my choice.
K ittens and puppies are not so funky!
E very pet is nothing compared to an ape.
Y es nothing is better than a vine swinger
S o there is a reason why monkeys are best:

T hey are tree climbers and banana bringers!
H ow do they do such wonderful things?
E ating and sleeping and climbing all day!
Y ou must admit, monkeys are really cool!

R eeking is something they do well but . . .
U nderneath though they really do rule!
L ove him; I really, really, really do -
E xcept he's my cousin's - monkey Maznu!

Mehajabeen Farid

A Trip To The Vets

It seemed like any normal day,
Nothing new on show,
I ate my breakfast, had a sleep,
Little did I know.

I like exploring round the house,
In and out of things,
So in the box I went to see,
Whatever I could find.

I trust my humans very much,
But I was a bit surprised,
When my sister followed in the box,
The door was closed on us.

I love my sister very much,
We do everything together.
We cuddle every night to sleep, and
Reassure each other.

The door was shut, and out we went,
Into the bright fresh air.
Into that funny, shaky box,
We bounced off up the road.

We stopped and out we went again,
Into a stinky room,
So many friends around us now,
All making such a noise.

This wasn't good, I had a feeling,
All these smells and noises.
Out I came, in Mummy's arms
And waited, eyes like saucers.

In came a strange man, smelling odd,
The humans spoke a lot,
I got flipped up on my back and poked,
Then Mummy lost the plot.

The humans seemed to talk a lot,
And give me lots of cuddles,
I felt my fur get cold and damp,
I didn't understand.

Next thing I knew, my mouth apart,
Some nasty tasting liquid,
Was shot into my tummy and
I felt like I was choking.

My tummy poked, they felt some lumps,
But they weren't hurting me,
They talked some more, why, I don't know
And Mummy cried again.

What was wrong? I asked myself,
I felt completely fine,
I don't know what they fussed about,
And why was I involved?

That night, we slept on Mummy's bed,
Curled up between the pillows,
That made up for the funny day,
All curled up together.

They forced my mouth apart each day,
And I swallowed down the liquid,
I pushed and scratched and fought at first
But they didn't take any notice.

Had I been bad? I couldn't tell,
Why didn't Pinky take it?
What had I done? I must think hard,
I won't do that again!

A while later, don't know how long,
Must have been quite a time,
Back we went, and saw that man
I was prepared this time!

I scratched, I fought, I didn't cave,
But this time, Mummy smiled,
No more yucky juice for me,
I got the biggest cuddle!

Charlotte Baird

Off To The Vets

Which one of us has to go
In that basket?
I hope it's not me - no . . .
Don't feel well enough to go
But she's bigger than me

Right, get the claws out - oh
Hind legs in first - I didn't know -
So I'm in
And off to the vets we go

Don't like that white coat
Or the needle he holds
Ow! - It's all over
And home we can go

Mm - now I feel better -
You lot better know
That if you feel poorly
It's best just to go
Get it all over, and back to the sun
Vets are there to help us -
Hello everyone!

Diana Price

Casper The Cat ... Casper The Friend

My furry best friend,
My object of confidence,
My companion to comprehend,
My symbol of divine providence.

He looks into my eyes with earnest respect,
I look into his eyes prepared to protect.

My cat is my comrade,
We are joint arm in arm in the face of every challenge . . .

He is a lot more than just my pet.

George Nelson Baldwin

The Companion

I wonder what you think,
as you look up at us humans standing over you?
Your gentle brown eyes constantly upon us,
Always eager for a word or a touch.

If we look for you,
there you are following behind,
or never far from where we sit, perhaps just out of sight
with ears ready in a moment for our voice.

Is it enough to feed you, play with you
or brush and stroke your fur?
Are we teaching you too, perhaps to be better than you are
as you have taught us to be?

What an intricate bond is this,
shared by mankind and the descendants of wolves.
We are very different species,
yet an impenetrable understanding bridges the gap.

Sacred is this connection,
hallowed by all who love the dog who lies by the hearth.
A mystical play on words reflects both
'dog' and 'god' so that each must mirror the other.

Yet we are poor gods for you, but you worship us still;
with all our frail humanities,
and our little vanities wrapped up in human schemes.
But you do not care for we are the best thing in all the world.

On dull days or through miserable experiences
you are always there, reminding us what it means to truly live.
With an inner contentment that a saint might envy,
and disposed to be as constant as the Pole star.

It is something of a miracle to commune with another creature
that has an ease of nature not known in mankind,
never minding what you do as long as it's with us.
Make us worthy of your unconditional, unquestioning love.

Stephen Austen

The Neighbour's Cat

Bounding along with his lolloping gait,
Very impatient; he doesn't want to wait.
The door is open, but who's that in front?
It's the neighbour's cat, who he usually shuns.
He hasn't seen him, but Jasper's still tense,
So he goes round the house to jump over the fence.

He's back in his garden, but far from relieved,
As there's another problem he's conceived.
Without any servants to open the door,
He'll just have to work even more!
That just won't do, he tells himself,
So he sits on the doormat and starts to yell.

Can anyone hear him? Is anyone home?
Maybe he should yawp instead of just groan.
Ah, that's good, his owner is here,
But it looks like she's waiting for James to appear.
He's round the front; quick, let him in,
He thinks he hears four paws on the bin.

A piercing miaow, a pleading stare,
But all Jasper can do is glare.
Now there's competition, how will he get in
Now that James is no longer on the bin?
Back round the front might be the key,
James isn't going in; certainly not because of me!

He says to himself as he leaps over the fence,
And avoids the grass and the flower beds.
Success! There's his owner; he's going to make it,
The corridor's in sight; he won't get missed.
But the door slams shut and guess who's behind him,
The letter box is open, but he's not that thin!

Lucy Martin

Suki (Whilst Still Alive)

I have a cat called Suki
She was rescued from a life
Of not going outside for five years
With chain-smoker husband and wife.

Son had asthma, so they put the blame
On his being allergic to the cat
But he would still be living with parrot and dog
And the smoking - no - let's get rid of the cat.

Before they had her they all knew
She had originally been found
Living as feral with nineteen other cats
They bought her for just one pound.

The PDSA vet said she was naturally thin
How old she was - no one knew
Definitely of Siamese cross
Had she been spayed? No one had a clue.

Lived with me now for two years
And still prefers to be indoors
Is brave enough to try outside
But, I still need to cut her claws.

Suki is still all skin and bone
But has a loud Siamese voice
Don't think she'll make a fat cat
But purring tells me I made the right choice.

Sheila Bates

Our Cats

They arrived in a cage two black, fluffy balls with beautiful questioning blue eyes
Two boys they were, their names, Tom and Jack, too soon we would say our goodbyes
We were fostering the pair, no way were they staying, keeping any more cats, no way!
Recently our hearts had been broken, at the loss of our Tammy, the pain felt we can't say

A telephone call followed with really good news, one sister had also been caught
Room for one more in the Grierson house, of course, just another new home to be sought
The cutest of kittens arrived at our door, ignoring the sweet face, our resolve it held fast
We reminded them daily this arrangement was temporary, and was never meant to last

Jess settled in along with her brothers, spitting and scratching quickly came to an end
Fun, games, ladders to climb, feathered toys to chase, their every need, our pleasure to tend
We followed this path for three more weeks, more fun, more cuddles and more toys
Another phone call said the final kitten had arrived, so still more cuddles, games and joys

The family were reunited when Wee Jean arrived, it was clear they loved one another
Looking after four was no harder than one so really it wasn't any bother
Thoughts crept into our heads, maybe one, we could keep, but how could we choose
Separating them for new homes would be hard, we knew what we all had to lose

So five years later it's with the Griersons they live, at least that's how it was meant to be
But we can't have explained the house rules very well, so it's often very difficult to see
Whether they live with us, or it's our privilege to jump to attention at their every need
Whatever the case, our lives have changed, and honestly it's our pleasure indeed

Morag Grierson

Poet's Dedication To Mr Tiger

Mr Tiger, my canine heart,
My faithful friend in Heaven,
That woeful day we had to part,
December 16, 2007.

For fourteen special years my loyal collie,
My extra shadow by my side.
Christmas 07 was far from jolly
Just nine days after you died.

You were sixteen weeks young when you first arrived,
February 4, 1994,
You brought a meaning to my life
At a time when the angels called.

And through the heartache of a loved one lost,
You became my faithful chum,
With those big brown eyes that always watched,
From dawn till day was done.

Fourteen special years we shared together,
Man's best friend and I,
Come rain or shine, whatever the weather,
You were always by my side.

Until dear one your time to part,
To leave this mortal shore.
Mr Tiger, you are in my heart
And shall remain for evermore.

Peter T Ridgway

The Joy Of Youngsters

We always had animals for our kids
The first was a mischievous kitten
They loved it to bits, wouldn't leave alone
Until they were scratched and bitten
Next was a puppy, a touch of allsorts
She was a giveaway
Didn't have to be bought
Then a canary my mother bought one day
Please would we look after it
She was going away
The cat sat and worried it making it die
Mum never got chance to say her goodbye
In the garden were hutches
For guinea pigs and rabbits
Collecting animals becoming a habit
Snowy the rabbit, albino by birth
Kept us in stitches proving his worth
Out on the lawn he'd drink tea from a cup
And wipe off his whiskers
After having enough
If you love children
You love animals too
Even if it means
You end up with a zoo

Daphne Fryer

Sheep Doggerel Anthem

Come rain and gales and whirling snow,
we've seen it all before and so
we raise a paw and swear that we
to farm and flock will faithful be.

In byres and yards across this land
you'll find our multifarious band
of collies who, though farmers scowl,
to pass the time this anthem yowl.

We may be muddy and unkempt,
and may have fleas and smell a bit.
We let folk in and then attempt
to bite their heels, we must admit.

But when the farmer whistles us
and duty calls, then with no fuss
we roll right through a five-bar gate
and all his needs anticipate.

We dip our tails and crouch nearby
to hear, 'Away!' or else, 'Come by!'
For we are clever, we're so bright
we know our left paw from our right.

That gate-roll is a skill innate
no other breed can imitate;
While other dogs are thwarted quite
we're up the mountain out of sight.

From puppyhood we know that we
were born to fetch from slope and scree,
from pasture, meadow, mountains steep,
those fascinating creatures - sheep.

Though some of us are less than brave
we teach those sheep how to behave,
we fix them with a glassy stare
and disobey they do not dare.

We yearn not for a life of ease
and only want the boss to please.
We're kind to ewes with newborn lambs
and stand our ground 'gainst bolshy rams.

The barn is cleared, it's time to shear
and men from neighbours' farms are here.
We know today admidst turmoil

we shall not rest from farmyard toil.
We'll work for hours and hours until
every sheep is off the hill
Oh lanolin, oh lanolin,
the smell of sheep all gathered in.

No matter how they shout and curse
(and some of them do even worse),
each farmer knows one truth of old:
a collie's worth is more than gold.

Though poodles sleep on satin beds
and we in barns and draughty sheds.
and when we die, in fields we lie
with grazing sheep above our heads.

Come rain and gales and whirling snow,
we've seen it all before and so
we raise a paw and swear that we
to farm and flock will faithful be.

Daffni Percival

Moving Home - A Cat's Tale

I had no say in the move, you know,
They just decided to up sticks and go.
Never mind the fact that I had friends,
A favourite tree,
My own territory.
No, my opinion was never heard,
If they'd asked me
I would have told them
The idea was absurd.

But wait, 'Who are you?' I hear you say,
Excuse my manners, I'm getting carried away.
My name is Leo and I'm like most cats . . .
Clever and kind,
And I know my own mind.
I live with a human family,
There's Mum and Dad
And then Charlie
Makes three.

So Charlie packed all his toys and his clothes
And soon enough we were ready to go,
I said goodbye to my favourite tree
And thought of our new home
Across the sea,
They called it France
And it did sound nice
But I had no idea
What my life would be like.

Our new house looked very grand indeed,
There was a garden, a pool and lots of trees,
Charlie could swim when the weather was nice
And I could play with
The local mice!
It may not be so bad,
I would give it a go
And maybe I would like it
At my new home.

One day I went to visit the neighbourhood cats,
I thought I'd say, 'Hi,' and have a chat,
But when I met them and said, 'Hello,'
They spoke in a language
I didn't know.

They did sound funny
And spoke so fast
I thought maybe I should
Just walk on past.

But I did not want them to think me a fool
And I did feel lonely with Charlie at school,
So I stuck around and listened some more
And soon the Head Cat
Offered his paw,
With a wink and a nod
We greeted each other
And I realised we did
Understand one another.

Then the others, in turn, all offered their paws,
They nodded and winked and said, 'Bonjour,'
First Pierre and Pascale, two tabby cat brothers
Then a white cat called Chloe,
Much smaller than the others,
They were scruffy and thin
And from what I could see
Not one had a shiny coat
Like me.

But they seemed very friendly and all in good cheer,
And I realised that I had nothing to fear,
The Head Cat had a name I cannot pronounce,
He spoke with a stutter
And walked with a bounce,
I called him Tom
And he didn't mind,
Wherever he went
The others followed behind.

One day we all met by the river's edge,
Their heads were down and they all looked upset,
I tried to find out what could make them so glum
Then I realised the group
Was missing one,
Where was Chloe?
Why was she not there?
Clearly this was the reason
For their despair.

As Pierre and Pascale did their best to explain
Tom wailed and whined again and again,
Chloe fell asleep on a bale of hay
Then the farmer's son came
And took the hay away
Across the river
To his family's home,
Now Chloe would be frightened
And all alone.

There were no bridges for miles around,
There was a road to the farmhouse through a distant town
But to travel on foot would take too long,
If we wanted Chloe back
Where she belonged
We had to act quickly,
And we were all very worried,
We had to cross the river
And we had to hurry.

Tom suggested we go to the road and wait
For a passing truck that was going our way,
I, on the other hand, disagreed
The road
Is a dangerous place indeed,
The trucks travel fast
And we are so small
The drivers don't usually
See us at all.

My friends needed help and I thought of a plan,
Now I just needed to make them understand,
With my actions I showed them we'd build a raft
And they stared at me
Thinking the plan was daft,
But soon Tom agreed
It was the only way
If we were to bring
Chloe home that day.

And so we all went to gather wood
And brought the biggest logs we could,
We set them down in one straight line
But how would we tie them
With no string or twine?
Aha! Tom knew
What would do the trick

And he set about stripping
Bark from sticks.

He used his teeth and then his claws
While Pascale held the sticks between his paws,
We tied the logs, Pierre and me,
And made a raft
Fit to sail on the sea,
With the raft in the water,
All the hard work done,
I shouted, 'Fear not Chloe . . .
For here we come!'

We were all aboard and the water raced,
We had to paddle hard to keep up with the pace,
But soon we came close to the opposite side
And this was it,
The end of the ride,
It was now or never,
We had to leap,
Though the riverbank
Looked very steep.

With a raise of our paws and a nod of our heads
There was nothing more needed to be said,
We all jumped off at the exact same second
The farmhouse in the distance
Beckoned,
For there Chloe would be
Afraid and alone,
Not yet knowing of our mission
To take her home.

We ran until our legs could run no more,
And there we were, at last, at the farmhouse door,
There was no sign of Chloe and the door was closed,
The least of our problems
As we saw who dozed
In a kennel just beside
The door,
Showing his teeth
Each time he snored.

Yes, there was a dog, the biggest I've seen
And even while asleep, he looked very mean,
We hardly dared breathe as we crept aside
And looked for a safe place
To rest and hide.

We found a barn
With hay and straw
So we crept in quietly
Through the open door.

As we considered what we should do next
And sat down to have a much needed rest,
We heard a sound we knew very well
Though where it came from
We couldn't tell,
Then suddenly Chloe appeared,
She was safe!
She grinned and cried
And licked Tom's face.

We were relieved to find she had come to no harm
As, united once more, we all left the barn,
I thought the farmyard seemed quieter than before
And I looked to the kennel
Beside the farmhouse door,
To my horror it was empty,
No snoring hound,
Then a menacing growl
Made us spin around.

Behind us one huge, ugly dog stood his ground,
His mouth open, showing teeth and drool dripping down,
Not a pretty sight for a peace-loving cat,
I quickly thought of a plan
While my friends hissed and spat,
I ran back to the barn
Knowing the dog would give chase,
And I hid in the hay
Watching his angry face.

The others followed behind, their claws now outstretched
And I gathered twine to tie the dog's legs,
As my friends ran around him he turned this way and that,
But he was no match
For five wily cats,
With our work complete
We made for the door
And when the dog tried to follow
He just fell to the floor.

Back at the river we had some luck
For floating towards us was a whole tree trunk,
If we timed it right we could hitch a ride
And use the trunk to get us
To the other side,
We made the jump
All safe and sound
And, after paddling hard
We were soon on home ground.

Chloe was relieved to be home with her friends,
And I was glad our adventure had a happy end.
I went home in search of something to eat
Then for a night and a day
I did nothing but sleep!
I had no say in this move,
You know,
But I must admit
I like my new home.

Karen Reece-White

A Day In The Life Of Me

I perch upon the TV screen,
Elegantly I proudly admit,
So my luxurious fur is seen,
For a queen I am fit.
I live my life at a quick pace,
As if I am living a race.

As soon as someone will open the door,
I leap outside and want no more.
When outside, I am on the prowl,
Disguised by towering trees,
My fur is browner than any owl's,
It shines as I waddle happily.

Hungrily, I gobble down my tea,
Tuna and chicken mixed in jelly,
Obviously everybody can see,
My food is of the highest quality,
Second best cannot please,
A royal cat such as me.

When the day is beginning to dawn
And as I compose a quiet yawn,
In my basket I shall sleep,
Not a miaow comes out, not a peep.
And until tomorrow comes,
You all can now see,
You have just lived a day in the life of me.

Rebecca Nasar (11)

Forever Friends

Big sad eyes and a wagging tail
To melt your heart, they never fail
A man's best friend - well that is true
They are always eager to welcome you.

Come rain or snow, they are happy to walk
Sometimes I wish that they could talk
I wonder what those 'sad eyes' would say
Would it be 'feed me' or 'come and play'?

My dog is always my best friend
A broken heart ... a lick can mend
Paws galore to make you feel good
Or a gentle reminder they are looking for food!

I couldn't be without my loving mate
To rescue him from the kennels was purely fate
Those sad eyes with his head on my knee
Confirm my dog will be there for me.

To all the dog lovers, just like me
I'm sure with my thoughts you would agree
Animal cruelty should be brought to an end
Your dog will always be 'Man's Best Friend'.

Lynsey Donaldson

Our Dog Chippy

Our dog Chippy is very old,
if he'd been a man
he would have a telegram
from the Queen.

He used to be frisky
and try to escape from our garden
which he did quite often
and annoyed the neighbours.

He loved to attack squeaky toys
but when the squeak broke,
he ignored them.
These days he only sniffs at new toys.

Now he walks very slowly
like an old age pensioner.
But he can still go for short walks
in the park and by the sea.

He cannot hear and cannot see,
yet he knows where to find
his newly filled dinner bowl
and empties it quickly.

Marrow bone biscuits are his favourites
and anyone who gives him one
becomes his special friend.
He even licks up the crumbs from the carpet
like a little Westie vacuum cleaner.

He sleeps most of the time
and is really quite boring.
Curled up on the couch
with his thick white fur
he looks like a big snowball.

Often when he lies asleep
his paws and ears twitch
and he makes funny noises.
We think he is dreaming
of chasing cats, which he hates.

Every year our mum says,
'Be extra nice to Chippy,
this is his last Christmas.'
Our Gran winks and jokes
that he'll see her out.

He has had several operations
costing our family a lot of money
which Dad is not too pleased about.
But we all truly think
that he is worth every penny.

One day soon we know that
he is going to die.
We hope he will be buried in our garden,
so we can feel
Old Chippy is still with us.

Helen Dalgleish

Skipness Morning

I shall dream of a Border collie
Chasing the dunlin
Skipping in and out, on the silvery edge of the loch at Skipness Castle
The dog attached itself to me for two hours one bright, sunny May morning
On the shores overlooking Arran Island, she joined me without any invitation
Just frolicked in the sunshine with a Jack Russell and
another collie dog, who later turned back
Yes she was my guide to the shoreline
Scattered with long, russet ribbons of kelp and discarded shells
Waiting until I caught her up then running on ahead, knowing every nook and cranny
Foraging under coconut, peach-perfumed, golden gorse bushes
Investigating a discarded rabbit burrow
Scattering sand everywhere as she dug a little further then off
Off once again chasing real and imaginary birds at the water's edge
Walking back in the hot, midday sun
Past the sweet mown grass of an ancient graveyard and church
Stone engraved flowers. Skull and crossbones stare out from lichen-encrusted gravestones
Ancient carved Celtic crosses nestle in boxes that only come
to the light as lids expose them to the sun's rays
Once more to hear the sea lapping the shoreline
A sound the stones remember
The collie is again joined by the other barking, a welcome or reprimand
But my faithful dog stays with me until back to the very spot she had joined me
So my guide would go no further
Her boundary line invisible
Only I say goodbye

Hilary Jean Clark

Index of Authors

We hope you have enjoyed reading this book - and that you will continue to enjoy it in the coming years.

If you like reading and writing poetry drop us a line, or give us a call, and we'll send you a free information pack.

Alternatively if you would like to order further copies of this book or any of our other titles, then please give us a call or log onto our website at www.forwardpoetry.co.uk